THE SECRET CODES OF HYPNOSIS

THE SECRET CODES OF HYPNOSIS

Spiritual Energy

George Spiric Fraxon

To order additional copies of this book, contact:
Xlibris
AU TFN: 1 800 844 927 (Toll Free inside Australia)
AU Local: 0283 108 187 (+61 2 8310 8187 from outside Australia)
www.Xlibris.com.au
Orders@Xlibris.com.au
818091

CONTENTS

§ Biography...vii

§ The Editor's Word...xi

§ Foreword..xv

1 Starting Means...1

2 Suggestion..17

3 Hypnotic Regression 37

4 On the Historical View.........................52

5 Ego 57

6 Spiritism..66

7 Telepathy...79

8 Significance — Truth or Obligation............93

9 Bioenergy — MIT or Reality 105

10 Clinical Death...124

11 Memory 138

12 Two Main Manifestations 154

13 Information and Its Energy Field...........170

14 Orb — Information Light Particles 193

Review 219

Foreign Words and Expressions........................223

Index...247

§ Biography

Yesterday it was gone, and it will not come tomorrow – only in the present moment is it there. 'We are also in this moment' is the mantra which best reflects the life and work of the author of this work.

George Špirić Fraxon is an independent researcher of paranormal phenomena and one of the most famous and best hypnotists in the former Yugoslavia. The current incarnation began in 1952 in Sarajevo. He spent his childhood and youth in his hometown, but his desire for knowledge led him to Ukraine and Russia, where he lived from 1992 to 1999. Staying there allowed him to gain knowledge of hypnosis as therapy. His education in Russia gained him the title of clinical hypnotist. His life path and desire for cadastral training led him to Australia, where he lives today. Occasionally staying in Thailand expands his knowledge and practical application of what he has learned.

Continuing to explore the distant East, he is also acquainted with the coexistence of Buddhism. His education and titles are of the wrong past, which no longer exists. It is a testament to day-to-day legality and values as incorrect or inaccurate. They are changing their new knowledge, discoveries, and achievements. Dogma wants to keep us in the chains of the hammers on the stump – every new change in the root is condemned, defamed, rejected.

Trying to regulate his thoughts and lives, Fraxon decided to study human behaviour and study the changing effects directing the developmental strands of each one of us.

In his childhood, Faxon's interest was related to the concept of being 'abroad'. He experimented with cheerfulness and educated himself in the direction of narrow parapsychology. However, the preoccupation of internal relationships prevailed. Therefore, as he was growing up, he paid the most attention to hypnosis.

His inborn (i.e. inherited) talent for hypnosis turned into work. He devoted himself to spectacles, making himself the first in the world to carry out mass hypnosis through the radio. He conducted his own experiments through the radio show *Golf* in Belgrade in 1994. Later, he focused on experimental and then therapeutic hypnosis.

The interest in the mental structure of a man and the functioning of his spirit requires constant research. He devotes a significant part of his work to the study of dianetics (the science of health) and the study of the aesthetics (a set of beliefs and teachings created by the literary fantasies of L. Ron Hubbard, who describes it as a religion which claims that humans are immortal beings who have forgotten their true nature), penetrating and manipulating human consciousness.

There was a connection between parapsychology and hypnosis with the samurai rituals of the Aborigines and the religion of Buddhism. The subject of Fraxon's research was the irritations carried out by the Masons, the influence of the ritual on the participants, and the creation of certain dependencies among the participants themselves. We add to this and to the study of the incarnation, which is under our veil of secrets. You will read about the results of these studies in one of the extraordinary books of this knower of man's consciousness and subconsciousness.

We should not neglect Fraxon's authorial project, Alfa Power. Namely, this is a meditative autogenous method developed by a mental hygiene specialist. The meditative autogenous method is used to achieve self-control and self-protection, spiritual peace, and the harmony of body and mind and contains breathing exercises, physical and physical disabilities, and hetero- and autosuggestion with acoustic accompaniment (twelve-megahertz musicians). Today this method is used by many wealthy people from world-famous businesses, well-known athletes, musicians, actors, and golfers from Australia and the United States, giving way to stressful life, negative influences, and trauma. The results of this method are a success – vitality in older age and effectiveness in the desired field of life. This method is slowly coming to Europe, while in the East, it has already gained popularity.

With special inspiration for research and development, Fraxon's work is located in the office and life of Nikola Tesla. He directs his work towards the detailed research of Tesla's life and work. In a sense, he is one of those who finds the connection between the scientific and the spiritual, which is still a secret for all but not for Fraxon as a researcher of the functional element of man under various influences. He investigated his psychological profile, mental complex, vision system, and procedures. He discovered how this worked with Tesla, which will be explained in this book.

Publicists describe Fraxon as 'an independent researcher of paranormal phenomena', which is plain but incomplete and shows only one and not the most significant part of his production. Among other things, he also discovered 'X points' of cosmic radiation or a portal which was written about by numerous newspapers around the world and which prompted NASA to conduct research in one location in the city of Niš. Namely, NASA has recognised and verified this invention, continuing to research and use real-time satellite imaging.

We could add another page of text in which we would try to answer the question 'Who is George Špirić Fraxon?', but the best answer to this question is going through the gates of time and the secrets in the book that is before you.

x

§ The Editor's Word

The truth lies within the firm, well-guarded ramparts deeply woven into our beings. Pushing into these depths and demolishing imposed boundaries opens the way to freedom of the spirit and true life.

The book before you did not accidentally find its way to you. It came to your hands as a result of searching for the truth and answering a number of questions that are as old as humanity, through which your being is covered. It is unique to the unmistakable respect of the truth and the courage of the author to communicate this truth.

Through an interview with a research team of scientists (RTS) which has been run on several occasions over a period of two years, the author presents facts from his rich work, life, and research practices.

By avoiding direct answers to very provocative questions, the author opens a new chapter in science and life knowledge. The well-grounded criticism very directly outlines the truth about 'secret knowledge', multi-time 'taboo topics', and demystification falsehoods of true knowledge, and those who use manipulative techniques have led millions of people into error, often impunity, bringing health and existence to danger.

He is very aware of his role and position. The author says that it is the Creator alone who has all the knowledge of this world – that is, to have all the information about posting and living – and that we are all mere seekers of the fragments of this vast corpus of information, by which we want to explain more closely ourselves and our role in this world.

The author's view of the world arose over a decades-long study of man, whose nature and legitimacy have been expressed and for whom official science has not given an explanation. One fraction of his knowledge, he has decided to share with you through the interview he had led with the RTS.

Courage is sharply criticised by the assumption that the results that official science has received are relatively accurate, some even far from humanistic orientation and sustainable only in artificial conditions.

Many of us have been taught in schools about what in real life does not exist, departing from the essence and the truth. We are bombarded with what St Nicholas calls 'excessive and diverse' knowledge, opening a wide field for consciously and unconsciously adopting delusions and untruths about ourselves and the world surrounding us.

In the book in front of you, you will find a handful of information that you know – but interpreted from a completely different angle. The author is openly talking not only about spiritism, psychics, clinical death, telepathy, and hypnosis but also about phenomena that represent the 'dark field' of classical science. A dictionary that is not intended for scientists, this book illuminates a portion of the mosaic, creating a clear picture of life, man, and space. The demystification of many world-famous mysteries represents the highest value that the author offers to the general public without annoyance and without awe.

Since the book began to be massively printed and distributed in a large number of copies, manipulation by 'knowledge' took a moment. The information was spread at a high speed with the development of media.

The river of false information runs daily and finds the way to each of us. It is very hard for people to resist everything, especially because they are 'packed' under the authority of their professions and science. This river is spreading everyday – pseudo-science, pseudo-religion, pseudonym, pseudo-art, pseudo-humanism. This book, unlike many that have overflowed in the market, offers the opportunity to come to the truth.

By giving answers to many questions, the author does not separate nature from the Creator, truth from the Creator, man from the Creator. He argues that truth cannot be seen fully, even scientifically, unless we involve the Creator.

However, knowing that the list of issues we face every day is not exhausted in this book, the author promises to continue and wants the light. Let's hold him to his word.

Academician Olga Zoric

§ Foreword

I'm not a writer, and this work that I write is neither a novel nor professional literature. It is not a niche work of art consisting of whimsical phrases, a description of the landscape, a dialogue of the main heroes. In fact, this is a testimony – that is, a testimony of the knowledge that I intend to share with you.

I am a witness and participant in the discovery of the 'energy (particles) of life', which give life to water, plants, animals, and every living being, from insects to man. The years of research behind me would have been wasted if I did not notice the phenomenon that had been practically 'in front of my nose' throughout humanity and which I want to share with you.

The question is, is this the 'Holy Grail'? This book is about the 'energy of life'. This book does not deal with the issue of any religion but recognises symbolically figurative and hidden messages from religious books which are presented in a wrong way or an inaccurate way. Some would describe this work as 'science fiction' based on religious and scientific grounds. I'm urging you to evaluate yourself.

Everything is based on exact evidence and examples. After this knowledge, you will be able to feel, identify, or decipher yourself. Where do we come from? Where are we going? How is a 'clinically dead' man alive? How do various 'paranormal' phenomena work? How and why is this happening? What kind of energy works around us and in us, without us knowing that there is anything at all?

Why are we 'blocked'? Namely, about 90 per cent of the potential of the brain is blocked, which is confirmed by official scientific data. How do we increase our energy potentials and put them in function at the present moment?

For many questions, you will find real and accurate answers within this section. The answers are different from all of it until now, but they are realistic and work according to some principles that you will be able to convince yourself about.

The material presented in this section is documented by facts and examples as well as live participants in experiments, photos, videos, visually registered records, frequencies accessible to hearing, physically sensitive vibrations, and specific results that you will be able to accomplish and check within yourself.

The book that is before you will give you a unique feeling that you are on the road of what you have been searching for for a long time. You will find answers to many questions. Step by step, day after day, your senses will be 'more open' to the world around you. Turning the page, along the page, you will get deeper into the hidden – actually, what has been there all this time – at your fingertips, but you had not noticed it because you did not know in which direction to look.

I want light for you.
The author

1

Starting Means

RTS: Can we answer with certainty the question 'Who am I?', go back to the beginning? Can you answer, first of all, this question by looking at yourself?

GSF: A difficult question. Who am I? You will receive the answer by reading *The Energy of Life*. In this book, you will find answers to who you are, where you are, and where you are going. To meet others and the world around him, man must first know himself. As I reveal everything, you will find out who I am.

RTS: You are, among other things, a hypnotherapist. How long have you been dealing with hypnosis? Why did you opt for this technique?

GSF: I've been dealing with hypnosis for quite a long time. It is important to say that I'm a practitioner and that I have a really huge experience. I was doing mass hypnosis in the big halls, where I encountered various reactions from people, from enthusiasm to great wonder.

I educated myself in Russia on this technique since I wanted to bring my express talent in this field into clear and very professional frameworks. I wanted to include it and the knowledge I had acquired for years to benefit the welfare of man. After years and even decades, I realised that people from whom I needed to learn more had limited knowledge. It turned out that the practice I had had was the best source of knowledge, an experience that was not described in theoretical books.

Over time, I have built my distinctive system – one might say 'unique' as each person has his own distinctive expression, so in myself, I have my own unique, completely original system.

RTS: You've been doing mass hypnosis. Can you tell me more about this?

GSF: I performed my first mass hypnosis session in the world through the *Golf* radio show in Belgrade in 1994. Already during the announcement for my hosting, we did a specially made jingle in which the message contained a subliminal message, i.e. the psychological preparation of handsets for a mass hypnosis session. I had to make a good idea of the whole concept because mass hypnosis has ever done through the media. I had no instructions or previous experiences, but I ventured into this challenge completely convinced of the success of the session.

Perfectly well prepared according to the plan and program that I had devised to the smallest detail and perfectly ruling the matter, I started with the program. The announcement and sublimation attracted so many listeners that the people themselves came to the studio, and the estimated listener count of the show was over ten thousand people. Then reincarnation was on the rise in popularity in these areas.

In line with all this, analysing the enormous interest of people for self-realisation, I came to the conclusion that the best topic would be hypnotic regression. The concept of the show was that the session lasted for forty minutes, followed by the direct involvement of listeners in the program to publicly hear their experience.

I expected subconscious listeners to extract deep-pressed stressful events or experiences from the past, but it happened that they entered deeper into a state (theta state), and the experience of the genetic code (the ancestors' experience) emerged. It was planned that the show would last for an hour. However, because of results and incandescent phones, all other shows were cancelled all night so that listeners could respect their interest and experience. People came to consultations the next day, followed by the interest of other media people. The results of this mass hypnosis were further roaming on other radio stations throughout Yugoslavia.

RTS: I wonder how you applied hypnosis during your rich experience.

GSF: Among other things, I have been working with painless delivery under hypnosis, hypnotic anaesthesia for easier surgery, painless tooth extraction, and support for introduction to total anaesthesia. What I particularly want to point out to better understand what I am talking about is that I am a clinical hypnotherapist. So in cooperation with doctors, classical medicine specialists approach the problem in a patient, and we come together to find the best possible solution.

Very often, at the invitation of medical specialists – such as cardiologists, nephrologists, neurologists, psychiatrists, otorhinolaryngologists, and other doctors, I would come up with a precise history, diagnosis, and, of course, solutions to help the patient in the best possible way. It happens that the specialist doctor would diagnose the patient and prescribe therapy, but it does not work at all, or it seems to work poorly in relation to what is expected.

In such cases, consultations with me are very productive as I am a clinical hypnotherapist with great experience, often having encountered cases where classical medicines were not of great help or partially resolved the manifested problem but not the cause of the problem and where the effects of medication gave poor and short-term results.

RTS: What, in fact, is the cause of human disease for you?

GSF: I could freely say that in the majority of diseases, there is a psychosomatic disorder. And this should be determined with a detailed observation of the patient, i.e. include professionally guided hypnosis and apply hypnotherapy in a full sense. In most cases, I have to deal with psychosomatic disorders first, and then I pass on to the effects of the disease. If we know the cause, we know the exact cure, right?

So hypnosis is not only a way to discover the causes of something but also a way to alleviate the problem or completely eliminate it. Hypnosis is a really effective painkiller. Unlike chemical anaesthetics that block nerve impulses that transmit information to the pain centre, hypnosis directly affects the pain centre. Hypnotherapy is an effective way of discovering the cause of the disease, i.e. various disorders, without chemical analysis and also treatment without the use of chemicals or other medicines.

I would especially like to mention that one of today's most widespread diseases of modern man, allergies, is very successfully treated by hypnotherapy, as are diseases caused by allergies, i.e. sensitivity to allergens.

RTS: How did you get to your hypnosis system?

GSF: I experimented and questioned the possibilities of man. I was wondering, for example, what can all be moved in a person in a state of hypnosis. Can it be psychic, whether it can be physically stronger, whether it can be smarter? Can it have a larger memory?

In Australia, in which I have been living for many years, I have worked with salty men. I wanted to know in detail their system of work. From a symposium, I wanted to 'take' the secret of knowledge and to get to most of the things they deal with. I had to be in their ranks.

I was interested in how they managed to make people literally 'wash their brains' and completely manipulate people. I was interested in these psychological processes and how it was possible at all to make a man give everything he has while still being satisfied. One read about everything, and the other one had all that in front of his eyes, in practice. It was interesting and almost unbelievable that a person put his whole life at the disposal of another person.

This experience has given me new insights about the power of acting on the masses. Mass hypnosis creates uncritical followers, fanatics, and addicts, but they can be recovered by the same method. In fact, at the time, through the media and hundreds of thousands of listeners who were following the shows I was broadcasting and who were at live broadcasts, I first realised that it was possible to program or reprogram a large number of people at the same time. I improved the technique I had used in the meantime, and today it is a unique technique in the world.

RTS: So first of all, do you put practice or experience 'on the ground'?

GSF: I was thinking of what kind of psychological process they are using to blindly obey. How can a man break a marriage, take all his possessions, and be a completely loyal follower? It all went 'like a badge', and I knew there was a programming technique for man, but it was kept well as a powerful weapon for collecting followers and completely managing them.

It was the only – that is, the most important – reason for my entry into this sphere and in those circles of society. I was aware that while I am in their ranks, I can discover many secrets and that it is impossible outside of their organisation. This is, however, only one segment that I dealt with. My research spirit and the desire to learn once brought me to the very edge of the gap, but I never gave up. The motive to help people is greater than fear, greater than any obstacle I have encountered.

When, thanks to hypnosis, you help a person overcome an emotional crisis or a psychological blockade that is very often a trigger for various illnesses, there is no cost. Curiosity and thirst for deeper spheres of knowledge, even 'secrets', led me to the knowledge that the state of hypnosis is one specific state in which the flow of thought is blocked by the recipient, i.e. the hypnotised person.

RTS: What then is hypnosis?

GSF: Hypnosis is promptly imposed by certain blocking commands or for the execution of certain actions. The person under hypnosis accepts this as his thought process and not ingrained, i.e. imposed. He thinks of this information, thinks, accepts, and thinks about it further.

Hypnosis, in fact, 'excludes' consciousness and creates new thoughts and flows of these thoughts. An entirely new personality can be created because a man often says, 'I think,' or 'In my opinion,' and he keeps those thoughts judging, working according to him, feeling, living.

So one can suggest thoughts that he will think of as his. Of course, I'm not just talking about possible abuse, which is possible while it is unethical. I want to say that with hypnosis, it is possible to reprogram man completely so that he thinks that this is his natural state of mind. Just imagine if such methods would be used in the resocialisation of criminal minds, for example.

RTS: What was your interest in, and how did you gain other experience and knowledge?

GSF: For over forty years, I've been researching the human psyche. Through all that work, I came to the knowledge that I started to check. I was particularly interested in how and why a man in extreme situations is capable of incredible reactions. A widespread case of a woman who managed to lift a 2.5-ton car to save her child is widely known. I will mention some concrete examples.

Angela Cavallo rescued her son who was trapped under a vehicle. At first, the woman did not know what to do but say, 'Help!' but help did not arrive as quickly as she had hoped. So she took things into her own hands – literally took the car and picked it up. Of course, she did not raise the car above her head but only a few centimetres needed to get her son out safely. It was noted once again as quite a miracle given that cars weighed over a ton.

Here's another example. Adam Simons worked on a routine brake service on his daughter's big jeep when the support poles were loosened, and the vehicle fell on him. After hearing her father's silence, Rachel Simons, aged 22, ran out of the house and picked up the car, weighing 2.5 tons. Rachel did not know herself and what had given her the power to lift a huge jeep.

And another example is when a certain Donna McNamee and Abigail Sicolo rescued a boy captured under a car weighing a tough 1.1 tons by raising the car themselves to get the injured boy under the car. They had stepped into a rescue operation when an 8-year-old boy was trampled in front of their homes. The boy, Bailey Fowler, screamed in agony after being trapped under the Renault Clio car. After they had heard the screams, Ms Donna McNamee, 24, and Abigail Sicolo, 29, ran out of the house, grabbed the car by the bumper, and picked up and saved the boy.

I've been thinking about these cases for a long time. I wondered what drives people to do things that are at their limit. It's a fascinating fact. A step further is the question of 'How it is possible?' The next query is if it was possible for these people to act in such extreme situations, is there a possibility that in some way, a second moment is produced, i.e. a situation is provoked in which they could do the same? Can such moments be initiated at all, and if so, in what way?

Various similar cases always made me wonder, and I studied such phenomena further as well as man's hidden possibilities. Earlier scientific research claimed that we use only 5 to 6 per cent of brain capacity, while the latest claims reduce this to only 3 per cent. This knowledge leads to the next important question – what about the rest of more than 90 per cent?

There are so many processes that occur in our body without our conscious control. For example, after drinking water, the process takes place without our influence. The same is with consuming food. A person consciously drinks water and takes in food, and further processes in the body occur without his will. Everything happens according to the metabolic processes in the body, without any further conscious influence. There is a logical question – can a man knowingly influence and exploit the transport of matter within his organism? We know from experience that this is not possible. Is that entirely correct?

It is also known that some people are trying to raise their awareness and that if they are successful, they would succeed in raising the level of utilisation of their brain's capacity by a small percentage. Then they have incredible memory and sharpness, make the right decisions, behave correctly in various situations. These are already familiar things.

However, is there a further step? What is the effect on the normalisation of blood pressure, the impact on the elimination of pain and its cause, improving vision, hearing? These are all questions that I ask. Of course, there are many other answers that I am constantly searching for as I discover the incredible possibilities of the human brain.

I was especially attracted by the question of how man manages to get an idea or how he succeeds in achieving something completely new, not a copy of something existing, and this can be considered a great scientific discovery. Nikola Tesla was my greatest inspiration when I thought about this. It is known that Tesla had more than seven hundred patents, of which about three hundred were registered in patent offices. This means that around four hundred inventions are not registered and that they exist only in his notes How he was and how he could have so many genius ideas are some in the series of questions that keep me thinking. Several times, during his few interviews, he said that through a vision, ideas turn into reality – that is, are materialised for the general's benefit.

Is there a difference in brain structure, as claimed by official science and with which I do not quite agree, or is it developing a special 'information reception' technique? I am thinking in that direction because I believe that the structure and characteristics of the human brain do not differ substantially but that there are significant differences when its use is in question.

It is also known that there are people who have fantasies, i.e. can fabricate things that cannot be proven, because their ideas are impossible to apply. Among many examples, it is also known that in the 1980s, students from the Faculty of Medicine in Belgrade, who were brought to practice by a girl from the Faculty of Electrical Engineering, posed various professional questions. Her knowledge of natural science was at an enviable level.

At one point, the professor asked the students about a car asking for patents. She began to talk about the principles on which car technology is based, referring to the unused potentials of water, hydrogen, and similar things in its visions. The students looked surprised and confused. A girl who was perfectly familiar with natural sciences had now talked about unimaginable things. The professor thanked the girl and told her she could go. He asked his young colleagues to give their opinions on what they had heard, and they stated their diagnosis. Most agreed that it was one of the 'F diagnoses'. Only a decade after that, world scientists began to explore the potential of hydrogen as a driving energy.

RTS: How are people watching today?

GSF: The vast majority of people, because of their limited abilities, i.e. insufficient use of brain potential, are often prone to such 'condemnations'. And those who could not understand what Tesla was doing and the way he created things called him a freak. On the other hand, there are people who are tempted to have 'opportunities' that are 'given to God' or simply 'possessed' by them. They persuade themselves and others to have 'power' and 'revolutionary ideas' that can change the world.

Such a thing can freely be called a paranoid messianic syndrome because such people, who are increasing nowadays, with their paranoid claims, destroy the masses. Often there is a late recognition of the futility of the idea of self-proclaimed 'messiahs', which, I can freely say, is dangerous to anyone they are addressing in any way, for the environment and other people and for themselves.

For Tesla, that's not the case. His genius ideas were largely realised. The first example is the alternating current, which is put into operation. Based on his discovery, we have light in the darkness as well as so many other things that drive the current. In Budapest Park, Tesla came up with the idea of solving the problem of alternating-current motors without a commutator while walking with a friend and reciting Goethe's *Faust*, whom he knew completely, and then suddenly, he started off with a stick on the sand to draw the lines of a magnetic force field. For the next two months, he elaborated sketches of many engine types and modifications that would be patented in America five years later.

His realisation of such projects has completely fascinated me. Now we have the internet, mobile phones, and many other things based on his theories, on something he was talking about eighty years ago. If we observe the philosophy that Tesla has brought light and heat to every home, it gives incredible strength and power.

RTS: In your opinion, what are they thinking?

GSF: We said that thoughts appear and that they can be subconscious, conscious, compulsive. Working with a huge number of patients, I came to the conclusion that the state of hypnosis, defined as an altered state of consciousness, is such that a therapist can insert specific suggestions or 'erase' certain experiences. I came to a concrete solution and an answer to the question of what is happening in that situation. The hypnotherapist succeeds in introducing a person into a certain state of relaxation, and in that condition, he only succeeds in stopping the flow of thoughts.

The concentration of thoughts focuses on the conduct of the exhortation he gives to the patient. So he assumes the role of thought, and the patient begins to accept the given suggestion as his own thought, not knowing in such a condition that he is the leader of that state and the information that is later transmitted only by the suggestion of the therapist. It is known that under the influence of hypnosis, we recollect incredible things, but it is also possible and completely unconscious under the influence of suggestion to see what, in fact, was not.

Hypnosis is, in fact, the state of hypnosis of thought or stopping the flow of thoughts and processing. Therefore, I conclude that thoughts are information we receive and which our brain only processes.

I speak about this from the angle of a hypnotherapist but also of a scientist. I can add something about thoughts – they are our guide. I'll give you another example. A person in prayer or meditation focuses his thoughts, i.e. he is in a specific state. When we deliberately manage to eliminate the flow of thoughts, we come to a state of complete relaxation, and this is one of the best things that can happen to a person. In fact, we can eliminate the presence, i.e. inflow, of any information.

Our unconscious receives a lot of information from our immediate environment, and we are not even aware of it. The barrier between unconscious and conscious processes is one of the so-called filters that prevent us from flooding information. From the preservation of the integrity of this barrier, our mental and physical health depends on our lives.

RTS: Does that mean that the brain is not the one that produces thoughts?

GSF: Yes, exactly, the brain does not produce thoughts. We think of information, a set of experiences, whether personal or genetically inherited, and the brain processes this information. I would like to explain something else here.

An infinite amount of information is broadcast through the ether as we have electromagnetic waves, which are information of shapes of certain frequencies and characteristics. The information we have for now on a special wavelength or frequency, which is timely – from the past, the present, and the future – this is information about our entire lives, with all the information from the lives of our predecessors, and this information goes through the air. This is usually called the collective unconscious.

It's easy to prove it. I will cite an example. It has been proven that water has memory. Water changes the structure of crystals, and under the influence of negative information, the crystals are deformed. Under the influence of relaxing music, they also change into the finest crystal structure. Water used in churches – also for baptism, for example – has the perfect crystal structure.

As water has the ability to store memory, so does the whole country have the same memory capability. Artificial memories for phones and computers were created from components that were removed from the ground – gold, silver, lead, zinc. The question that follows is why then could you not remember all the elements of the country? These elements have incredible quantities in the country itself, and they are also able to store information.

So through the ether, an unlimited amount of information constantly circulates. Man is actually just a receiver. Our brain receives information it can process. We only influence thoughts in the information field and get information that interests us. We cannot get much because we are blocked, but we can also get a lot of things. A man often says, 'I think that's it.' This does not necessarily mean that its processing of information is accurate and that this information is positively effective on that person.

RTS: And what happens when we sleep and dream? What is then with our thoughts?

GSF: The brain in the state of desperation, as a receiver, receives information that it 'finds'. We are all unique 'receivers', and no other man on the planet is like us. The information we receive, the brain processes and transforms it into images – that is, into a dream that is uncontrolled. In addition to all this, many external phenomena affect man. So it is with the influence of the celestial bodies that move, even the moon. We are sensitive to these external influences of the cosmos because they are in an interdependent position with the earth, where many living beings and man, of course, live.

A man is exposed to various information that he filters and processes selectively. If we are talking about short-wave radiation, the source of which lies outside the solar system and whose frequencies measure less than one hertz, these wavelengths are of the order of several million kilometres, and their energy is barely measurable, yet we get this information.

The fact is that the shapes of such low-frequency waves are almost impossible to distinguish from waves that an electroencephalograph can record in the human brain. Among the mass of information that the human brain receives, four basic forms – alpha, beta, delta, and theta – are distinguished. Of these waves, the slowest motion takes place in the delta wave, one to three cherubs and the easiest to record during deep sleep. Such waves have a frequency of four to seven hertz and are believed to be related to our mood.

Many experiments were carried out on this occasion, and the deviations in the measurements were minor. Alpha waves are most commonly reported at a time of relaxation or meditation and have a frequency of eight to twelve hertz. They can be disrupted by directing people's attention to something else, i.e. by sending some information. There are also beta waves, which have a frequency between thirteen and twenty-two hertz and are related to the frontal area of the human brain, in which the most complex mental processes take place.

The most widespread are delta waves on the frequency between 0.5 and 3 cherubs. They are recorded in newly born children and appear in traces until the end of the third year of life. Delta waves are characteristic of the state without thoughts and the influence of external stimuli. They are also reported in people suffering from some types of brain tumours. In the yogistic state of meditation, *samadhi*, it is also possible to record waves of this frequency. With monks in deep devotion to prayer too.

When we take all this into account, we come to the question of how many unexpected waves still exist, i.e. channels through which it is possible for the human brain to receive information. Is there, in fact, a reliable way of steering, controlling, or blocking information? Of course, here I am not talking only about manipulative techniques that affect man's thinking and doing but also about a more complex question – how does the human brain receive and process information? I devoted my whole life to this type of research and finding answers to all these questions.

RTS: Can we go back to the hypnosis process? I wonder how it comes to one.

GSF: Hypnosis is often confused with sleep, i.e. the state of sleep in which the hypnotist is guided. Hypnosis is a specific condition for which no one has yet found a precise definition and full explanation. Even those who, throughout their lifetime and the scientific age, have repeated this phenomenon have never managed to clearly define the situation.

Russian psychologist Ivan Pavlov considered it to be a kind of defensive mechanism similar to sleep. On the contrary, Uruguayan physician Anatoly Milehnjin describes hypnosis as an emotional reaction that is achieved by provoking shock, i.e. some sudden audio or palpatory stimulus. Stefan Black, an English psychiatrist, claims that hypnosis can be a reflex condition that occurs early in childhood. Many, I say, were trying to define hypnosis, its causes and processes as well as the effects.

A large number of studies have been written on the topic of a kind of trance because of the effects of music, i.e. audio information from the outside environment, that served to put one under the control of the hypnotist suggestion. In fact, you want to ask me about the irritation of 'falling in' certain conditions.

It is mainly hypnosis that involves patient-and-hypnotherapist cooperation – human hypnosis. The patient accepts the hypnosis method to improve his health. The basic task of a hypnotherapist is to help the patient gain confidence and to make the patient almost sure that after therapy, they will be well.

RTS: This was related to the individual or hypnosis of one person. And what about mass hypnosis? There is no consent of the masses. The first time you did mass hypnosis, as you have already mentioned, it was on the radio, and there was no consent of the people who were under the influence of that process.

GSF: Consent does not have to be given, but still, situations like that of the individual are the same. They can also be produced by the masses.

It is important to be well prepared, referring to sublimation that works so that people gain conviction or the opinion that we want to produce with them.

Group hypnosis is happening, and people often do not know it. Likewise, there are group hypnosis sessions through which people go voluntarily, either from the need for new knowledge or from curiosity, or there is another reason for this, such as hypnotherapy. They start from the leader of the sessions, the medium, and spread like an infection.

Mass hypnosis is sometimes easy to work with in relation to the individual. It is important that patients are well prepared, but of course, much depends on the skills of the medium, i.e. the hypnotherapist. The hypnotherapist must clearly convey information without external influences, i.e. physical irritation that would be de-concentrated or something that would be influenced by the external environment so that the information it conveys is not crystal clear to the one to whom it is addressed.

2

Suggestion

RTS: How would you define a suggestion?

GSF: Suggestion is the process of open or secret guidance by one person or group of people to accept ideas, beliefs, attitudes, or particular patterns of behaviour uncritically but without compulsion. This conviction is manifested as a suggestion, address, or command. This information can be clearly stated or in a covert manner. Suggestion is often used in therapy as well as in economic, political, or any other propaganda. To put it more simply, suggestion is information that someone imposes on an individual, group, or mass in a visible or hidden way, directly or indirectly.

The suggestion, therefore, can be communicated or 'inserted seamlessly', can be sent directly to an individual or through an intermediary. It can only apply to an individual, but the reaction of an individual can cause a chain reaction, and then we say that it is addressed directly or indirectly to a group of people. This information commands the execution of certain actions or convictions to perform certain actions by an individual or a group.

In the modern era, suggestions can be even of a promotional character, thus convincing consumers about the quality of the various types of products that can be found on the market. If it's heard in the advertisement – 'Buy this and that so that you can do it' – then there is a command-line message. Therefore, it is command-line character and represents an order that should be executed.

In addition to marketing, suggestions can be applied in the military and politics. We are exposed daily by suggestive attacks. The same is happening in private everyday life. For example, between two lovers, when one of the partners suggests to the other how they should behave.

RTS: Is there a link between suggestions and subliminal messages?

GSF: A thin thread divides suggestion and sublimation. Sublimation is a contemporary form of effective suggestion. Autosuggestion is specific information that a person personally entrusts to himself, and he suggests a certain desire or intent to function according to the message he suggests to himself. Let's say that he is not afraid of the darkness, that he is not nervous, tense, angry, etc. It is an order that we give to ourselves to make our subconscious in certain situations order us to act in accordance with what we have given ourselves by autosuggestion.

Post-hypnotic suggestion is the one that is subsequently executed. Such is the case with the medium or the person who is introduced into a hypnotic state when a post-hypnotic suggestion is given to her, i.e. an order to be in any situation anytime and anywhere, all after the hypnotic process.

Post-hybrid suggestion is sublimation with information that should be performed also later. The recipients of non-hypothetical suggestions can be masses who, through a medium, such as TV, follow a certain show or a particular advertisement. When they meet with a particular product, when they go to buy bread and on the shelf see a product from advertising, they purchase the bread product.

The most important key point in suggestion is that the recipient clearly receives information, comprehensibly, then it is clear, concise, and understandable, without foreign words or dialect, so that it is immediately accepted. Therefore, it is essential to have a good knowledge of the language of the person to whom the suggestion is directed. For a successful suggestion, there are keywords that act as a trigger. The techniques of the interview draw out the words of the respondents to get familiar, acceptable keywords. When analysing the language of the medium, the person, or the mass to which the suggestion is directed, the keywords that can trigger are used. If it is a matter of religious suggestion, in which we would cite Christianity as an example, the suggestion would say, 'In his lectures, Jesus said that we are doing good to return to us well.' Let's assume that this is a positive suggestion, which aims at spreading good among people.

Judging by this, we will say that the suggestion can be positive, negative, and commercial. It is interesting that every human action can be the result of suggestion, such as a command or an imposition. This is not the decision of the one who receives the suggestion but the imposed information, the imposed order which should be executed. Always the subconscious is ordered in the suggestion, receives this information as important, as something that should be done, and at that moment, the order is executed.

Sublimation is the most advanced type of suggestion. In principle, it is an order that is not direct but indirect. Suggestion can also be visual. When we see a particular situation or a photo of behaviour, we imitate what we have seen. The best example of this is fashion. Fashion is shown through photos with very little text. A visual form of suggestion and imposition of fashion propositions to be adopted is given.

Today sublimation is present in commercials, and so we have one famous brand of carbonated drinks whose advertisements had sublimation to our invisible eye. To see the movement, i.e. picture or film, for one movement, twenty-four frames are required. Marketing puts sublimation as the twenty-fifth image of your brand name. The brain registers but does not have enough speed to handle the information because the following thumbnails come in, and it stores all that information together with that twenty-fifth thumbnail. Then as I already said, the consumer goes to the store to buy bread and on the shelf sees the product he saw on that advertisement and buys both the bread and the product. Without knowing, he puts it in the basket, with the intention to decipher the message of the advertisement.

Sublimation gives information that we consciously register, but we do not have time for conscious analysis and analytics. For example, if we hear music, there is a message posted on the channel that is recorded at such a speed that it is barely heard as a mumble. This gives our subconscious the task of resolving what is mumbled and the message behind it. The subconscious recognises this but does not return the information back to the consciousness. When sublimation is well designed, it is great for athletes as well as for hypochondriacs, people who think they are sick.

The subliminal message works instantly the same moment when it is heard. Repeating listening to such messages is embedding commands and repeating them until a system of habits is reached. For example, at some point, we get a habit of consuming a famous brand of carbonated drinks, or if we take into consideration the fact that smoking is a habit and not a necessity, then the use of certain cigarettes is suggested.

The secret to the success of suggestion is in the application of keywords which are used as a trigger. The most common are archaisms or words that are of interest to persons of a particular age or completely new, fictional words very similar to the common name of a product. As such, the suggestion is embedded in our nervous system. We think it is correct and respected. During the suggestion, we can use an unlimited number of words. However, fewer words containing the suggestion are more effective. It can be reduced to even one letter.

RTS: Should the suggestion be written or pronounced to be adopted?

GSF: We have already said that there is visual suggestion. It contains a photo with little text, which is most often followed by the appropriate slogan. A thin thread lies between suggestion and sublimation.

A suggestion is direct and concrete, and you see and hear it and even feel it in vibrations. It can be musical. In rare cases, it can be sublimated. A suggestion can only be a series of tones. An example is a siren for an alert, which suggests that there is imminent danger to human life. A suggestion can only be a picture. The simplest example is a traffic sign or a traffic light, which suggests how to behave in traffic.

On the other hand, a sublimation is an unclear message, but it also has a keyword or an audio or video recording, but it is set up or sent in a different way. Sublimation recognises only the subconscious, which receives it as an order to process later and execute.

We have negative suggestions or sublimations in an infinite number of examples. For example, there are politicians who manipulate the system, as Goebbels did, in a negative sense, which was propagated on the basis of a system of repetition, embedding keywords and triggers, marketing positively directed towards Hitler. They had managed to deceive millions and millions of people around the world. A good politician uses these methods in his speeches and serves with specific words and certain messages, even gestures that are strong suggestions in conjunction with key triggers.

This form of sublimation is also observed in presidential campaigns before an election. Sublimation has evolved to the maximum in a visual sense, and through good graphic design and photography, a certain sublimated message is passed. Visual sublimation is especially used in politics as well as in the economy, in marketing, where everyone seeks to make better and more successful sublimation, i.e. they send suggestions with the intention to improve their business, i.e. come to profit.

They say that everything is allowed in love and war, and in contemporary society, this is true for business. The question that arises is whether it is ethical and humane. This is already at the court of time that will show how much information is manipulated, i.e. sublimated messages of good for civilisation. For some, this is the only way of 'survival' for mankind.

RTS: Whether there is suggestion and to what extent it determines a person's life, how does this, in practice, affect the course of his life?

GSF: Suggestion can positively affect man, as can autosuggestion and sublimation. It affects human health. It feels good and healthy to eliminate sadness, depression, neurosis, fears, etc. Very successful suggestions are applied in hypnosis as well as post-hypnotic suggestion, which man subsequently executes. Many, not knowing the perfection of suggestion, make big mistakes and cause greater problems for people than help them, which is achieved through various analyses.

For example, in numerous astrological interpretations, certain information and suggestions to people focus attention on phenomena and objects, even if they are not aware of it themselves. The result of such a process is to determine the behaviour of a person based on a horoscope, which can be positive but also very negative. Often it happens that astrologers are not aware of the perfect process of command and execution. They approach the laic one process of sending information, which can negatively affect one.

A man can receive suggestions visually or through listening and even smelling. It is found, for example, in the army, and their uniforms are, by no means, infused with mothers. When a person, after twenty to thirty years, experiences this smell and hears a certain order which is not a military type – for example, 'Give me a cigarette!' – then the order would be executed without thinking.

The sense of smell relates to information that remains and results in the mechanical execution of the action. Our memory retains everything that the eye has seen, the ear heard, the nose smelled, the mouth tasted, so all our perceptual senses are remembered and connected with the orders and events. A man can also receive a suggestion in the state of sleep, in the alpha state, and, of course, in the waking state.

The most successful suggestions work when a man is tired. Then they are the most effective. The 'fatigue of the material' leads to a reduced resistance to the execution of a specific command. The effectiveness of the suggestions of political speeches tells us a lot about it. We know that Hitler held speeches at night because Goebbels knew that in the course of a day, a man broke with thousands of information and his defence system would not be able to assess whether something was good or not because it was minimally active during the evenings.

The ideal situation would be when a person sleeps and at the same time hears suggestions or sublimations. So-called passive learning is a technique that is applied in such a way that during the night, while a man is asleep, certain messages are transmitted to his brain. At first, he will not fully comprehend everything he has 'heard' during sleep, but in time, these messages will result in the fact that in a fully conscious state, he reproduces everything that his brain received during sleep.

RTS: Are the sublimated messages permanently masked or concealed, or after a while, can we also discern both such messages as those made as a suggestion?

GSF: Sublimation is always hidden, and a person does not know what is in the message that comes to him, which means he is acting secretly. Unfortunately, many psychologists, psychiatrists, psychotherapists, and self-styled psychotherapists can leave extremely negative suggestions that can cause problems in the patient, i.e. the recipient of those messages.

As an example, we will put together universal suggestive messages. The primary program that man operates is the maintenance of life, which requires high-quality foods full of vitamins and minerals. Because of this, the food industry gives special emphasis on the composition of the products, which are the basis of vitamins and all necessary substances important for human health and vitality.

If we are speaking about targeted information, for example, when two heads of state speak, then the whole team compiles messages that will bring them together. Unfortunately, the mass of self-healed healers and prophets leaves a very negative post-hypnotic suggestion that is constantly working, and their clients are constantly visiting them to solve their 'problems'. They do it consciously and, very rarely, unconsciously.

The success of sublimation depends on whether there are keywords or key information that can be triggers. The defence of imposed sublimation is consciousness. When we are aware that such a thing functions around us and that we are being attacked in such a way, we involve analytical awareness. Our mind analyses that information and recognises that it is an order, a sublimation, and whether the answer is something we need or not, whether it is good for us or not.

So it does not matter who tells us anything or why they tell us this, but it is most important what is told to us and whether it is what is good for us. A familiar and popular form of sublimation is signs and symbols. All the famous symbols are the flags of states and then religious symbols and then the logos of companies, and they all send out a particular message.

The power of the symbol can be so strong that people worship the symbol. The simplest form of successful character communication is the language of the characters communicated by deaf people. One sign can mean more than words, so it is evident that communication with signs is recognisable. Even in some cases, it has more power than a written or spoken word.

For example, the sign of the Mercedes when we see it speaks much more than we could explain. This sign is a set of all the information we've heard, read, or seen about the Mercedes. Another example is the flag. The flag of a country is a symbol that carries a message about that country and is also a trigger for all the information we have learned about that country. The power of symbols and characters is strong and effective. It affects both the consciousness and the subconscious of man.

We can conclude that these techniques and methods can significantly affect human behaviour, i.e. his conscious and unconscious manifestations of behaviour. They can also be extremely positive for human health and mental health, even for healing. Activating the self-healing system in man, we can run with positive, well-conceived, studiously concentrated key information. With this system, many well-known psychiatrists achieve excellent results.

RTS: On what principles does autosuggestion work?

GSF: The human brain is constantly processing a large amount of information. It is one of the properties of the human brain that it can receive and process a great deal of information. Accordingly, man is different from other living organisms – i.e. has what they do not – say, amoeba.

At first, immediately after birth and up to one part of life, each of us grows up with people who are significantly older than ourselves and who have experience – that is, already adopted information about themselves, about us, and about the world around us. Over time, a person experiences different experiences, and on the basis of 'overcome problems and limitations', he acquires autonomy in decision making and individuality in thinking, i.e. making conclusions, decisions, about their movements, i.e. on the road and the like. All this time, our brain receives a great deal of information that piles up and forms a glimpse of the world as it is seen by every individual for itself. Our mind works for the rest of our lives, continuously complementing and processing all that information on the basis of which the processes take place on a daily basis, and at the same time acquires certain experiences and autonomy.

At its highest level, our brain processes all the information entered and draws conclusions, even when there are no external incentives. This is the situation when we say, 'I was left alone to think about it.' Hence, a person often 'speaks with himself' during his or her life. That is, he thinks, makes some conclusions, and imagines, and wishes that are not instinctive appear. This man works in a conscious state. These processes are manipulated by a CNS.

However, his unconscious works in parallel with the conscious. This unconsciously represents much more than a part of the brain that deals with physical physiology. True creativity relies heavily on the unconscious, and this is supported by numerous statements by famous artists who often wrote their best works in a 'fever', i.e. 'between java and sleep'.

Autosuggestion, if used for positive purposes, can be very effective in humans every day, even medicinal for the human body. Unfortunately, autosuggestion can also cause negative consequences for your psyche – that is, the mental and physical health of your entire body. Negative autosuggestion could be explained in many cases, but I will give the simplest explanation.

Some psychologist 'predicts' that he will lose a beloved person in the near future. A person subjected to an unreserved belief in the claims of this 'seeing' person begins to think intensely about it. He is wondering if a loved one will actually leave him and in what way, whether this refers to abandonment or death. He starts checking the beloved person to question everything about the information he received from the 'psychic'. It is increasingly difficult for a person to gain control of his conscious actions aimed at examining the information received. As he is occupied by it because he is deeply convinced of the truth of the 'psychic' claim, he begins to function differently than usual. He begins to persuade himself that he has to do something to prevent it.

So it suggests that something works. This is reflected on not only him but also on his environment. He, constantly dealing with misinformation, makes a series of irreconcilable and illogical manifestations of behaviour which disturb his entire psycho-physical state. This can lead to minor but also significant consequences for that person. A break from everyday routine behaviour does not go so easily unnoticed from the environment, and there are feedback reactions which again affect an individual.

In some cases, de-concentration, pause, a permanent feeling of concern, and sometimes depression or even fatal outcomes may occur depending on the web of circumstances. Therefore, misinformation in conjunction with autosuggestion can cause a series of negative consequences for the individual and his environment. The same happens when an individual 'convinces' himself that in some cases, he is destined for failure or that some situations will have bad outcomes. Just transmitting such information to the ether has its negative implications, and they return as boomerangs whether they want it or not.

Autosuggestion in the negative sense for us is nothing but advance condemnation of ourselves for some failure. People of the pessimistic spirit are more inclined to do so, but they need to be honest and say that this is a characteristic of man and that we are often suspicious of our ability or the outcome of some event. We can create this negative environment which, if we do not overcome it, can go in an autosuggestible way of thinking and even acting in a negative direction.

Man's brain is a powerful machine that can recognise this as a mistake and 'bring us back' on the right path, but subconscious actions that result from negative autosuggestion can be fatal to man. However, autosuggestion can be extremely important for the individual and for his environment. By autosuggestion, i.e. by the information given to ourselves relating to a process, it is possible to achieve things that we thought were impossible in our 'case'.

Often we hear from someone, 'I knew I would succeed!' This is nothing but a joyful exclamation of the one who has inflicted himself in a kind of positive autosuggestion. 'I will succeed. I know that I will accomplish this. That is my path. I will do it. I will heal. I'll get it.' There are countless examples that each of us can point out from the experience of other people and even our own.

It is, in fact, about positively directed information to ourselves about a process that is of great importance to us. By suggesting to ourselves that we go to someone 'through success', we are hiding our way to ourselves. An individual who has autonomy in thinking, positive experiences, and expressed individuality can achieve a number of positive desired results with autosuggestion. The experience of successful autosuggestion opens up an individual with a higher level of awareness of himself and the world surrounding him.

Those who are prone to negative autosuggestion turn around in a vicious circle, and they need the help of a therapist, a good knower of how to get him out of that vortex before he 'sinks'. Unfortunately, an individual is often unaware of the causes and all the bad consequences of this negative autosuggestion, so he often knows to ask himself, 'Why are all these bad things happening to me?' But in most cases, he cannot get himself out from the whirlwind that he has made for himself. Therefore, when it comes to autosuggestion, we must keep in mind what 'tasks' we are giving ourselves and in what way.

Autosuggestion defines the goal or the meaning of our lives. If it is positive, it is very likely that the life of an individual will be 'directed' in a positive direction. Negative autosuggestion can often lead to unwanted consequences, to depression, or even to serious illness.

Three hypnosis stages are known – alpha, beta, and theta. All these states have substations or subcategories and are categorised in degrees. All these conditions are very individual, and each person, the medium, in different ways, enters the same, which depends on the current psychological and emotional state and the psychological profile of the medium.

The hypnotherapist, by a certain suggestive method, introduces a person into one of these states, and he becomes a guide and takes over all the commands. The media or patients in the state of beta are relaxed but still aware of the surroundings, sounds, and situations in which they are. The status of the state is stepped up, and the person feels a greater degree of relaxation while in the fifth and sixth degree of beta, in the alpha state.

The characteristics of the alpha hypnotic state are complete relaxation and the stepwise absence of consciousness, but the critical mind still functions. The hypnotic stage is already the absence of consciousness and the critical mind, and the hypnotherapist takes on the role of consciousness and becomes the main guide.

The beta hypnotic condition is the one in which the process of preparing the medium for hypnosis is done. It is a conscious state in which the fear of getting into hypnosis is eliminated, and trust in the hypnosis and the condition that follows as well as the safety of the consequences is instilled.

In the alpha hypnotic stage, in which there is still consciousness and a critical mind, there is a confirmation of safety from the consequences of hypnosis and a change in the state of consciousness, and because of the pleasantness and acquired confidence, the initiation of a desire to continue the process is initiated.

In this state, there is complete relaxation of the body of the person, complete muscle relaxation, which indicates the fifth or sixth degree of the alpha hypnotic stage. Already at the fifth and sixth degree, communication is possible between both the hypnotherapist and the medium, and the situation is not to be disturbed. It is possible to initiate memories of past events and reproduce them again. In this stage, it is possible to completely extract from the person what the person wants, a problem that is troubling, and all the answers about the quality of life that he is not aware of.

The theta hypnotic stage is already a complete lack of consciousness and a critical mind, and the hypnotherapist takes on complete guidance. Communication takes place between the medium and the hypnotherapist. At this stage, a hypnotherapist is able to enter the deep memory of a person and obtain all information that the medium has subconsciously – for example, a traumatic event that is completely suppressed by conscious memory because of great pain and trauma.

Also, at this stage, it is possible to enter the memory field of the medium in which information and ancestors and their lives and events are located. Only a genuinely talented and expert hypnotherapist can extract this from them because he must have a high level of sensibility to be able to guide the person to this information and distinguish, select, and censor information from real, genetically coded, inherited information or from experienced information from films, various roles, and identification with them.

In this state, it is possible to detect traumatic events or stressful situations that are deliberately suppressed, which act as a trigger for psychosomatic diseases, from depression to cancer. The biggest advantage is the elimination of these triggers that are in the subconscious and have led to illness or various conditions. This condition allows the person to initiate the self-healing process because there is full availability to activate it and put it into operation.

This state of affairs is very suitable for post-hypnotical suggestion, and it is a program that is 'built in' and runs later and can last a lifetime. It is a trigger that has led to certain conditions. This new 'embedded' program can be crucial in the process of curing psychosomatic diseases and various other conditions. The program is very powerful and effective, and unfortunately, it is often abused. Through many years of work, I have often met with the results of the abuse of post-hypnotic suggestion.

I would like to mention here the conscious suggestions of people of various profiles and professions from the highest levels, such as religious figures, politicians, doctors, lawyers, astrologers, mistresses, interpreters, sects, religious fanatics, and, what is most prevalent for all ages, everyday advertising materials. These suggestions led many people into impassive and helpless situations where they would encounter both the deepest depression and fully channelled views of life and would solve all these cases with success, even if the medicine would be declared as hopeless cases.

It is absolutely certain that post-hypnotic suggestion and hypnosis lead to the solution of many states and concepts because the subconscious manages life, not consciousness. In recent times, various 'philosophers' appear – lecturers who, with their knowledge, do not bring people into confusion for profit. By their suggestion, they lead people to the wrong attitudes instead of solving the deeper path of the problem, so in reality, we have a very small percentage of people who come up with the promised results, with suggestions, and the majority of those fall into even bigger problems and do not find a solution because of the implanted suggestions.

As a classic example of the abuse of post-hypnotic suggestion, I pointed out that in 1982, I had already revealed the appearance of the famous lady from Medjugorje. It was then that I was banned from telling the truth about it, with threats to my life. Today my discovery has been revealed that this is an abuse of the power of group post-hypnotic suggestion. They are programmed to receive visions of the perception or hallucination with the lady in a certain ritual. After the publication of this discovery and detailed explanation in the media, after two weeks, the pope announced that they did not recognise the 'phenomenon' of the lady from Medjugorje and that all the gatherings were urgently suspended after my explanation and the pope's confirmation. Finally, after more than thirty-four years, the truth came to light, and the people ceased to be deceived for selfish interests.

RTS: Individual hypnosis is the most common practice? How is it implemented?

GSF: Individual hypnosis or clinical hypnosis is used to treat psychosomatic disorders and disorders. With my experience, I realised that there is a close connection between the subconscious and the body. The body is therefore behaving according to programs that operate from the subconscious, but when these 'bad' programs are eliminated as dominant, their influence ceases, and the self-healing process is initiated, the proper functioning of the body and organs.

Also, individual hypnosis can be applied in treatments in which group hypnosis is applied. The best results are obtained precisely because it is possible to determine the cause of the disease as well as its time of origin. Telepathic communication is very intense between a client and hypnotherapist. However, what is also important is the charismatic hypnotherapist's knowledge and experience as well as a special sophisticated sense of recognising at the moment the state and degree in which the client is located and identifying a successful keyword for suggestion. It's never the same because no client is the same.

I will cite an example from my practice in Australia where my client found an acquired epilepsy from which she was unsuccessfully treated for about fifteen years. The first attack was in her twenty-eighth year, and since then, she has received attacks several times a day regardless of the medicines she has consumed under the instructions of the doctors. In seeking help in Switzerland, America, and Australia, she came to me.

I got her into a hypnotic state and discovered the cause of her fascination, but it also led to immediate healing. Namely, in her twenty-eighth year, she was operated under a blind hose. Having received a minimum dose of anaesthetics, she came into a half-conscious state in one tentacle in which she felt pain but she could not react. Also, she heard the cuffs of the instruments with which the doctors worked. From that moment to the end of the operation, the epilepsy began.

In the hypnotic state of my treatment, we came to the cause – that is, whenever she heard somewhere a specific sound that was resonant with that of the surgical instrument and attached to the instruments, she would experience epileptic seizures. That sound was a trigger for entering an indefinitely unconscious state like that under narcotics and therefore was physically blocked by any reactions. But it happened in restaurants, at home, in public places. That's how my client's long-term problem was solved very quickly forever.

RTS: Is group hypnosis another of the hypnosis praxis modules?

GSF: Group hypnosis is used in the treatment of drug addiction, alcoholism, and other forms of addiction, sexual frustration, behavioural disorders, hysteria, speech disorders, night watch in children, phobias, and fears as well as the lack of confidence.

Mass hypnosis is practiced at religious and political meetings, in the media, in marketing, and for military purposes, and it differs very sharply and is used as a sublimation system, which is a kind of perfected action of hypnosis. Sublimation is effective, and since a person cannot consciously register with his senses, he cannot even influence its action, so he always falls under its influence.

RTS: You are the right person to ask how mass hypnosis is being conducted. How is it applied and who is applying it all and why?

GSF: I have already mentioned that I have performed a massive hypnotic sample in the world through the *Golf* radio show from Belgrade in 1994. This experience has given me new insights into the power of action on the masses. Mass hypnosis creates uncritical followers, fanatics, and addicts, but they can also become aware of the same method.

RTS: Self-hypnosis is a process that is also known in practice. What are your experiences?

GSF: Auto-hypnosis is a process that we initiate and implement by ourselves on ourselves for the purpose of self-therapy. This process does not achieve the same results as those in the process when a hypnotherapist carries out a classical process of hypnosis over the patient. The process of self-hypnosis on a person, provided that he knows how the process of hypnosis is achieved, can be carried out by repeating itself or by listening to a targeted image.

The state of auto-consciousness differs from meditation, although this is similar to it. At the very beginning of the process, its duration is programmed, and the necessary or desired autosuggestions and the number of repetitions are targeted. It happens that the auto-hypnotic state automatically goes into the delta state or sleep state and lasts as long as it takes the human body to rest.

The results are obtained when a person independently, without expert advice, programs the whole process based on many books on the market, which often have the wrong tips or are weak or non-existent. They can lead to confusion and even negative consequences that are later difficult to remove.

From personal experience, during many years of working with clients around the world, I came to the realisation that energy is an information tool that produces various states, of which each state has its own stage, in a human being. Apart from the state in which a person can be brought in by the directional energy of the information, he can act in a waking state through a program with the system of hypno-sublimation. So in the state of sleep, the delta state, it is possible to program a person and imitate certain suggestions. Information can be sound at different frequencies and vibrations. It can be a voice, a word, a single tone, or a set of tones on a particular instrument and the cries of animals, birds.

Information is not only sound. They can be directed as various scents, flavours, softness or hardness, touch, temperature, colours. These are important for the processes of the situation that we have talked about. All senses work on the principle and system of information, and each of these components individually represents that energy information. All these components are very different in the processes that we have stated to be complete and harmonised.

All this needs to be taken into account for a successful client outcome. Many self-taught 'therapists' and also highly educated professional medical staff are not aware of the importance of all the components listed. By applying all the components and properly conceived information, working with clients, I came to fantastic results.

Knowing the tiniest shades and details of the method and its functions, I conceptualised my 'alpha power' method, the same kind of training I hold all over the world, through which life in a positive direction has changed a large number of people. Many of them have solved their psychosomatic problems, fears, depression. The communication system in this case, when it comes to communication between the hypnotherapist and the client, where the hypnotherapist is a transmitter and the client a receiver, is precisely determined by the information.

RTS: In the current practice of a hypnotist and a hypnotherapist, it is known that it is possible to establish hypnotic anaesthesia. How does this work?

GSF: Hypnotic anaesthesia is the term for surgery in which the patient is under sedatives using hypnotherapy instead of traditional anaesthetics.

Hypnosis for anaesthetic purposes has been used since the 1840s, when it began to be used by surgeon James Braid.

During hypnotic anaesthesia, the hypnotherapist brings the patient into the delta state and thus achieves complete control of the reflexes of the patient in a certain part of the body to the level of anaesthetic action so that pain in the traditional sense is not felt. Patients are aware of the feeling and often describe a tingling sensation where otherwise the pain is felt. Hypnosis is used in pain management, for controlling cramps in the muscles or during rehabilitation.

What is more commonly used is a combination of the hypnosis regimen and a local injection of analgesics, i.e. as a mild sedative. It is administered to patients who are elderly or other persons who have increased the risk of general anaesthesia. The patients are under sedatives and brought to a state of increased alertness by listening to a story in the operating atmosphere.

Anaesthesiologists at the University of Liège in Belgium performed more than 4,800 surgical interventions, mainly ORL and thyroid glands, over the past ten years. The main benefit of hypnotic anaesthesia is that it has fewer side effects, and in general, the patient can leave the hospital earlier than when anaesthetics are used, and less blood loss is evident. Also, post-operative nausea has been reduced.

3

Hypnotic Regression

RTS: What is the knowledge of contemporary mankind, and how do we regain the independence of the world through 'myths'?

GSF: There is great popularity of the quasi 'hypnotics of aggression' starting from the thirtieth year of the thirteenth century, when ethical sessions were conducted in noble societies as a form of entertainment. Later, it also reached even greater popularity and encompassed broad popular masses. With the passing of a series of books from the popular psychology that gives instructions for sessions, how regression can be traced back to past lives, it becomes very popular for humans to look at everything unknown.

In the same way, many other members of the family were able to learn the source of the course, trained, and cured sick people, most often with paranoid guru syndrome, representing patients with regression therapists. Self-employed regression therapists – most often on the basis of popular literature, which is often very stuttering and even full of misconceptions, or on the basis of courses led by unskilled persons in the desire to quickly gain money and population – are recruited in regression therapy. Such persons, on the basis of the acquired 'knowledge and skills', engage in regression therapy, and this is very dangerous for the patient.

In the meantime, in the same way, in the first place, in the same condition, the people of 'past lives' have instructed the people of the country to live 'like' the other, the female candidate for the life of the incarcerated. The information obtained in the case of any of the abusers is susceptible to the desire for certainness – the hero, actor, nobleman, etc. In the absence of such a book, the so-called therapist of a person does not understand the position of the person or patient.

In this process, it happens that certain information is randomly registered, but it is not processed completely or in the right way. They also report a variety of forms of confrontation or confusion and the activation of the phobia, in the past, on the age of the law, and among those who are suffering from the consequences of the victims – the healer, the psychologist, the 'parapsychologist', the wizard.

RTS: Do you still need to register the process and the damage to your cell or your device?

GSF: Clinical and diagnostic procedures are processed with the test results. In such a process, it is possible to discover the cause of the disorder as well as the precise time of the action and the way to solve the problem. The disease of the lungs results in the occurrence of a virus, thanks to which the disease of the liver is activated, leading to other attacks – cardiovascular, asymptomatic, epileptic – and various malignancies in sexual intercourse, affecting potency or the orgasm, such as the sterility of women.

To clarify the course of regression therapy, it is best to compare it with a movie tape or a film that is full of events and experiences that each of us has. The regression therapy procedure takes place according to the script that was written by our life, and by returning to certain sequences of that scenario or film, the regression therapist discovers the causes of certain manifestations that manifest themselves as disorders or illnesses.

I will mention a number of examples on the mood of the subject as a result of the work of the leader who is in the same position as the author. The clinical highness of the registry is the same as the one in the past year. They tried to get themselves in the way of the money. In the meantime, they even reported themselves when they crossed the floor of a laptop. Since then, it has not gone to the sea, nor is it in the vicinity of water.

Discovering the threats, hypnotherapy is the minimum of the offender and even the other. Strongly successful and brilliant in the face of a woman, it exhibited mostly sterility on a psychosomatic basis. In these cases, it is essential to include the event of the load through the technique of the carriage. Frigidity and potency are among the fastest-looking problem-solving groups. There is an infinite number of examples that can be stated, and most importantly, the problems are permanently solvable.

You asked a question on whether hypnotic regression can hurt. It can leave lasting consequences if it is led by an inexperienced person or someone who is considered to be an experienced regression therapist. It is classical abuse that can and should entail legal consequences for itself. Why do I say that? There are several reasons.

The first reason relates to the very process of 'guiding' through regression – that is, a return to an earlier time or a pre-state in which the cause of the manifestation of the disease or the psychosomatic condition of the patient is sought, i.e. the trigger for health problems. If the patient returns to the condition and the time in which the trigger for the problems develops and is not guided by a professional regression therapist, he can experience real horror. Facing the causative agent, the so-called trigger, completely unprepared to cope with it at the moment can cause additional problems that later greatly cause deterioration of the general state of the patient or even lead to new health problems.

The second, no less important, is the reason that once so badly managed, regression therapy leaves consequences that, later, are more difficult to correct and represents a much more difficult task both for the patient and for the experienced regression therapist. Fixing an 'error' does not mean just a lasting process but also dealing with a number of problems that mask the real basic problem.

The third, also negligible, reason is the loss of patient confidence in regression therapy, which is one of the basics for removing the cause of the problem. Faith in healing is as important as just the treatment – that is, therapy. Therefore, the risks of poorly managed regression therapy are multiple. It should not be neglected that poorly managed regression therapy can be a real-time loss in the patient's struggle to lead a normal life or even a battle for naked life.

And of course, there is also an economic effect, which I personally do not consider so important, but of course, it should be mentioned. The patient unnecessarily uses a certain amount of money to something that either does not work or acts contrary to the expected and desired. All these are more than enough reasons for carefully choosing a regression therapist before literally turning one's self to his hands.

RTS: What happens, actually, to us during hypnotic regression?

GSF: No case in practice is identical. First of all, I want to say that there are basic principles, steps, which are followed by hypnotic regression but that the approach and process itself is different from case to case. Basically, the most important is trust, discretion between a hypnotherapist and a patient. For each patient, the responsible regression therapist keeps a proper record – that is, a personal card of the patient. In addition, the whole course of regression therapy is recorded and delivered to the patient. And these are confidential data that are subject to regulations and should not be misused.

Bringing the right reason to submitting to such a very complex process is very important. Only after establishing mutual trust and a clear clinical picture can a hypnotherapist enter into a process that, in a word, represents 'searching for a needle in a haystack'. An experienced hypnotherapist is initiating you and introducing you to the past, confronting you with the cause, the trigger, and your problem.

I know it sounds complicated, but it's a kind of state inherent in two-time events. I emphasise that this is a very complex state through which we pass primarily mentally, but it is strongly reflected and manifested in the physical condition of the patient. It is therefore very important that hypnotherapy is professionally led. Clear manifestations of the disease, regardless of whether they are of concern – asthma, epilepsy, stuttering, night urination, migraines, dizziness, or some other health problems – should be established. Only then should the introduction into hypnotic regression and the search for the trigger or the cause of the problem take place.

Each person distinguishes a 'state and level' of consciousness about himself, the world, the environment, and so on until reaching the very nature of the problem itself. This knowledge is very tangible, completely individual. An experienced regression therapist starts from this point of view, not from one that is general, common to all. An experienced regression therapist is primarily guided by the fact that each individual is a world in itself.

RTS: How does the process of hypnotherapy from the patient's perspective look like, as well as that from the angle of the hypnotherapist?

GSF: You should know at the outset that a symbiotic relationship is established between the patient and the hypnotist. The hypnotherapist must enter the patient's psyche. It is necessary for the patient to be professionally prepared with regard to information on the course of regression therapy, achieving absolute confidence, etc. The patient must know that at any moment, he can rely on a hypnotherapist throughout the process.

In the process of regression therapy, the most intimate secrets are revealed as well as suppressed unconscious information. Therefore, a clear boundary between the patient's angle and that of the hypnotherapist cannot be withdrawn. Why? Because this is a kind of 'joint time travel', necessary for understanding the causes of the problems that have arisen.

Throughout this process, mutual respect, harmony, and understanding of the patient and the information received are required, as well as focusing on the most important details. It's often a way of communication that has not been known to the patient until then. In fact, the 'navigation' of the patient is performed on certain suppressed experiences. He focuses on them. He keeps his attention on certain phenomena and re-survives them.

Often, during regression therapy, there are very strong emotions, like pain and euphoric conditions – wailing, laughter, aggressive behaviour. In this repetition of the event, the regression therapist must not allow the patient to 'exceed the limit' – that is, the patient is too exposed to the trigger – but not alleviate the confrontation. This, perhaps, is one of the most sensitive segments of regression therapy because the regression therapist must adapt to each patient and his abilities or how much he can tolerate and, in doing so, get the best results.

RTS: Do you mean that a hypnotherapist is, to a great extent, identifiable with the patient?

GSF: Yes, they are identified somewhat, but first of all, they take on the role of their guide. To be a good guide, a time and space navigator, you must be familiar with both the *time* and the *space* in which you are moving, i.e. get involved in the 'ambience' of the patient.

Let me explain. It is not a mere identification but a common passage through space and time, an information time gate that opens when entering the process of hypnotic regression. This entry through the temporal gate represents nothing more than a two-time manifestation. A small dose of carelessness, or, god forbid, ignorance or inexperience can be very traumatic for a hypnotherapist but especially for the patient. It's about collecting information from the past and putting it in the context of the present.

The process of gathering information itself is a kind of trauma to the patient because he is in a kind of way going through the time in which the so-called trigger occurred for the problems that are manifested in the present. In this way, the patient, together with the regression therapist, faces the cause of the problem. And this confrontation is sometimes physical pain, a sound, a trauma which is repeated. Just confronting the trigger is a repeated trauma but also a way to find the cure.

It is important then to have a good guide with you, a good regression therapist who will point out that this is just a necessary process of 'repeating the historical experience' from which one needs to move on, a step towards the lasting solution and troubleshooting. The session is very dull because it lasts for hours and can be repeated up to 120 hours total until the moment of discovering, creating an engram, a trigger.

Many of my patients were completely exhausted several hours after regression therapy, as if they were running a marathon, which is perfectly normal. After that, the feeling of relief and victory was the dominant feeling in all. I have to admit that I have felt the same way countless times. It is this symbiotic feeling that is established between a patient and a regression therapist that is not inherent in classical medicine. Harmonisation and alignment of the rhythm and feelings of the patient and the hypnotherapist is a basic requirement for the success of the sessions.

RTS: Can you give us at least some examples that you have faced in your practice?

GSF: I had treated a person with sterility and frigidity. A 38-year-old woman asked me to help her solve the problems that had been torturing her for a long time. After receiving basic information and the preliminary interview, I accepted working with this patient. She was ready for cooperation and unreserved openness, which is a condition for work that gives results.

After the first session, I was already on the trail of the cause of the problem. I would not go into the flow because it is a confidential and complex process, but I will say that I found the cause of the problem in the patient's early life, i.e. in the period when she was still a baby. Namely, by 'returning to the film', the patient remembered the scenes where, in fact, there was a problem. Her parents, having ignored the fact that their newborn baby was nearby, were very loud in an intimate relationship.

The next 'trigger' in close association with it was a bloody stain on her parents' bed, which the patient saw at a later stage of early childhood, and brought her in line with a previous experience. An additional aggravating circumstance was triggered by the mother of the, patient who spoke to her with a great feeling of disgust during the period of puberty so that she should not enter into intimate relationships with a man before marriage as this can have exceptional consequences for the health of my patient.

By collecting all these situations, by 'returning to the film', I uncovered several engrams that led to the result – frigidity and sterility. The symptoms that had first emerged were painful intimate relationships, discomfort, fear, disgust during and after intimate relationships. In one word, the real nightmare was the patient's intimate relationship. Incidentally, for the first time, she had entered into an intimate relationship at the age of 27 with her husband.

Psychosomatic sterility also appeared as a secondary phenomenon as the physiological findings of the patient indicated a gynaecologically healthy person. Frigidity and sterility have been the result of early childhood engrams and upgrades during later life. Spotting, identifying, and confronting this act was a step towards solving the problem.

After successful regression therapy and the instructions that the patient was following afterwards, she became the mother of two children. We are no longer in contact today. This certainly means that all the problems have been solved successfully. I would also say something related to this case but also to the emergence of frigidity that is very common or the impotence that occurs in males.

During the regression therapy, a cause is required, i.e. all the information that led to this kind of disorder, whether it's frigidity or impotence. A very common cause of frigidity is the reception of information from the outside world, from the immediate environment, about the sexual relationship treated as a disgusting, blasphemous act, something that should not be practiced before marriage with more people, which can cause unwanted pregnancy or illness.

A person who receives and adopts information that is related in such a way to sexual intercourse has a kind of fear and repulsion towards himself. A sexual act means the merging of two people, the sharing of both the physical and the psychological parts of one with another person. The mystification and 'muddling' of such a kind of very intimate relationship is caused later by various disorders such as frigidity or impotence. The sexual act is something quite natural that happens in the living world and even between people. It's a sensory process. So they are also involved – but as a rule and emotions.

The disclaimer of a completely natural instinct and sensibility is like giving up the need to breathe, see, hear, taste, or smell. By adopting such information about sexual intercourse, the attitude and the person's awareness of this act changes. However, this is not enough. They must first confront the causative agent which has led to the manifestation of problems in the form of frigidity or impotence and then only adopt new information that it is a completely natural and normal process that is part of our nature.

The one who adopts such a way of thinking fully accepts his nature, his physical and spiritual being, and is able to function smoothly. Only a person who fully accepts himself can accept another being. He can love one word in the full sense of the word. And to love or to express positive emotions towards oneself and others is a condition for the physical and mental health of man. The absence of this kind of feeling, acceptance, and giving of love to the environment leads to various disorders and diseases and is very often at the base of each one.

Impotence is a very similar thing, unless it is a question of a physiological barrier or a dysfunctional disorder of an organic nature. Most people in the male sex are afraid of some of the earlier events or information that have influenced the belief that the sexual act itself is something that can cause various negative implications for that person. In a very similar way, regressotherapy as well as frigidity or neorgans is caused by infertility. The most important thing is to spot the cause and correct it properly with the right information that solves the problem.

RTS: So successful regression therapy is carried out of several individual therapies or fundamentally prepared sessions?

GSF: That's the way it is. However, one needs to know that from many factors, it depends on how much time it takes to prepare and how many sessions it takes to complete the entire process completely and lead to the desired results. We should not ignore the fact that the preparatory phase is of great importance for successful regression therapy, regardless of whether this refers to the onset of work with the patient or the period between two regressotherapy sessions.

These preparations include the collection and processing of as much information related to the patient, the specificity of the manifestation of the disorder, i.e. the illness, the definition of the most suitable term for the session, the duration, approach, and way of working with the patient, and the like. The process itself during the session is complex and very specific and depends on the case, i.e. the general health condition of the patient and the complexity of the disease.

I will also note that someone needs more breaks during one session, for example. Also, the time interval between two sessions is a matter of individual nature and an arrangement between the regression therapist and the patient.

RTS: How long does it take to achieve successful regression therapy?

GSF: There is no answer to this question expressed by the number but as a statement – on ways should be required to cause the discipline and successful octals. Why is it so? I have already said that the preparations, the number of sessions, and the time between two sessions are of an individual nature. I say this on the basis of, someone would say, a huge number of clients who went through my office.

Many trained, not to say incompetent, regression experts claim that ten sessions are enough for each client to 'process' – yes, to 'process' – financially but not professionally, therapeutically, and to solve the problem that is successfully detected and resolved. I apologise for so much harshness, but I believe that already marketing information about ten regressotherapy sessions, which have their own tariff, is abused and misleads many who need help.

To this, I will give you an example from your practice, which is one of the most complex and specific cases I have ever had. There was a male who had lived in Sarajevo during the civil war in the former Yugoslavia, one of the areas most exposed to the war situation. For my help, his daughter addressed me in the time I had lived in Ukraine. Although very few people knew at the time where I was, she tried to find me.

At first, when she had told me about who and what was left, I was left alone. The person in question is my acquaintance or someone who was my neighbour for many years before I had moved to the other end of the world. In a telephone conversation, I had already learned from his daughter about details related to the event that had caused total amnesia with side effects. I told her that this is a case that requires a special approach and probably a long period of treatment.

Not giving up so easily, when she had finally found me, the daughter suggested that her father be brought to Ukraine and that she would remain as much as necessary because they had no other solution after having visited all the doctors and surgeons in the past ten years in an attempt to help and observe a small positive shift in the treatment.

Just fifteen days after our telephone conversation, she came with her father to Ukraine, where I then stayed. Before me, I had a man full of white hair, white eyebrows – remarkably, unnaturally white, with a silver glare. From the conversation with his daughter, I had found out some of the details related to his present condition.

Namely, during the war, he was in his mid-war zone in his house, from which he had to occasionally exit to perform tasks related to basic purchases for home use. One day he found a sniper as he moved along the usual route. In search of shelter, he threw himself into the nearby ditch, shielding his head behind one stone. However, his body was exposed to the sniper rifle. For more than ten hours spent under the sniper rifle, he had twelve bullet wounds. The neighbours found him the next day and transferred him to the first medical checkpoint. At first sight, he did not have salvation because he had abundantly been shot at, but with some miracle, he managed to survive.

His hair and eyebrows, every hair on his body, lost pigment. They became completely white, de-pigmented. However, after stabilisation of the condition and the first visible signs of recovery, the closest family members came to visit him at the doctor's call. Their call was sent to identify the person they had treated. The family were then faced with the embarrassing fact that he had completely lost his memory about his personal identity and could not recognise anyone or remember their names.

Emotions that are implicit in someone having acquaintances and friends, especially close family members, had completely disappeared because the person whom he had met after the accident had only his first name and was presented as someone who had been in his life before something meaningful. So emotions towards close family members did not exist in the extent and manifestations that are common for a balanced human mind. Simply, they were strangers to him, as well as all the others he had ever met in his life. It was very painful for the family, but their great desire to help him recover at least some of his personality was enormous.

At the very beginning, I knew that a huge job awaited us. I talked to him for days. He understood that he was talking, judging, reading, writing, taking care of himself, and thinking, but he could not remember anyone from his previous life, even his childhood, his origin, his marriage, his children. I gradually directed him to remember the details of the accidents that were crucial to his condition.

The sessions lasted just over three months. The trauma he had experienced left an incredibly deep trace. The cause of his amnesia was related to the person, the man who had inflicted evil on him. He, a very characteristic, benevolent person, could not even imagine that someone could torture and gradually deprive one's life for hours. It was the main trigger that removed from his memory all that was related to persons – their names, all the emotions related to any person. His memory was completely empty in terms of people.

After long-lasting work and success to regain complete memory, he returned with his daughter to the place where he had lived. Shortly thereafter, they told me that the pigmentation of his hair began to return. I was trying to explain how it is possible for people to completely relieve themselves in a short period and then how everything gets back to their original state.

The chemical process occurred in his organism as a result of enormous stress, i.e. fear. He had made it completely in all the battered areas. The phenomenon of pigment return can only be explained by the fact that information related to the release of fear has again made some kind of chemical process that affected it. However, this case is one of my specialties in my decades-long experience. Not only by the complexity of the procedure that I had to apply but also in all other manifestations that followed my patient's condition from the first to the last session. It is rare for a person to be born twice as the same person, but in this case, it can really be said that it happened.

RTS: What, in fact, is the cause of total amnesia in humans?

GSF: Although most psychotherapists would say that there are different causes, I am responsible for the basis of a large number of cases claiming that amnesia is an interruption in the acquisition and channelling of individual information about the self and the world surrounding it. It's about the code for communicating with a certain piece of information that we own and that is simply locked up.

The cure is nothing more than restoring this code for communication and establishing a connection with the experiential information – that is, information about the self and the world that surrounds us, i.e. all the information we previously adopted. For such a process, as I have already said, it is necessary to establish a very professional and studious approach with a person who has a problem, a well-planned and guided process of regression and patience. This can be a process of gradually recovering information or simply returning a code to restore all information at once. It depends on a case-by-case basis.

Any information that is 'saved', segment by segment of a lost mosaic, must be carefully calibrated in case of the gradual return of information and the establishment of their correct flow. Neither one nor the other approach is as simple as it seems at first glance. The choice of which method to approach is crucial for the success of regression therapy. That is, for comparison, as if you are using medicine in the treatment of a disease like pneumonia. If you are treating your lung cancer with a rheumatism, it can have negative implications and even lead to the death of the patient. That is why, once again, it is very important to whom you 'give up in your hands' or who performs regression therapy.

4

On the Historical View

RTS: Your study of hypnosis is very fundamental when it comes to practice, which, of course, involves knowledge of the theory. Can you tell us more about the history of hypnosis that is known and, of course, what is covered by the general public?

GSF: The history of hypnosis is, according to what I have encountered, analysing the written and 'swallowing' all that has come to my mind, full of contradictions. Hypotheses of different authors often get away from the essence. That's what confuses people. On the one hand, the history of hypnosis is a bit like the history of breathing. Like breathing, hypnosis is a feature inherent and universal which all human beings have been experiencing since the beginning of humanity to this day, very often not knowing about it.

On the other hand, in the last few decades, we have realised that hypnosis has not changed for millennia, but our understanding and our ability to control some processes have changed quite deeply. The history of hypnosis, if considered from this point of view, is nothing but a history of change in the perception of the hypnosis process itself. I believe that all this sounds pretty confusing, but it's quite simple.

RTS: I have to admit that everything you say is a little confusing but at the same time encourages an even greater desire to clarify what hypnosis is, how it works, when it is known, and whether we are all hypnotised in the same way. Through the history of civilisation, hypnosis is linked to secret learning and the knowledge of 'chosen ones'. Is it knowledge that can be learned by studying the literature and with the good guidance of an experienced teacher?

GSF: Suddenly, you ask so many questions, but I understand your desire to get to the knowledge that has floundered for thousands of years. Yes, thousands, probably for millions, no matter how difficult it was for us to think in such a way and in such a long time. Human knowledge is, in fact, precipitated by the existence of consciousness. This can also be said for hypnosis, although there is no material evidence. When I say material evidence, I think that it is always easier for a person to believe in what he sees, hears, and touches that in what is claimed.

But I believe that you have heard of the optical illusion, prejudice, imposed thoughts, misconceptions. That's the case with hypnosis. People will sooner believe if they are provided material evidence of the existence of something than face the fact that there are some immaterial things, as there is air that we inhale. Has anyone ever seen the air? No. Has anyone ever touched the air? No. However, the air, for all of us, exists despite us not seeing it, touching it, not hearing it, right? Do not think that I'm moving you away from the answer. On the contrary, we are approaching the essence.

Is our opinion really ours? That is, are our thoughts really the product of ourselves? Or are they collectively imposed, inherited, taken over, ingrained? We could interpret it in different ways. I will only say that hypnosis can be achieved, whether individual or collective. We must know that the mind is above the material.

It is known that even philosophers in ancient Greece were trying to divide the matter into smaller and smaller parts, while Democritus did not categorically claim that there was a limit after which the particles became invisible and atomic, i.e. indivisible.

Two thousand years after Democritus's claim, John Dalton, an English physicist and chemist, put forth the hypothesis that all matter in the universe is composed of basic material elements, the smallest particles, i.e. atoms. Modern civilisation believes in this claim. But is that really the case? Do not be confused. You heard about 'splitting atoms'? Here, you see, it's still possible to split atoms into smaller particles, to those dimensions that a person has not penetrated with his observation. Only some modern scientists claim that there is clear evidence that nuclear particles, which carry the mass of atoms and energy, vibrate as a wave form.

Tesla spoke about this over a century ago, although he did not have such precise laboratory instruments. But Tesla's 'instruments' were more perfect than those we can meet today in the most modern world labs. Scientists who follow a 'classical' school are still far from real cognition. They are trapped in the adopted 'illusion of knowledge'. On one hand, I can agree with those blindly following the course of the universally accepted scientific corpus. Life is closely related to matter. However, at higher levels of organisation of life and matter, energy supply and information are constantly interacting.

Hypnosis is an old secret knowledge. It is not learned. Before, you could say it has been perfected. And it cannot be used by anyone but only those who have the 'code'. In the twenty-first century, there are still those who see hypnosis as some form of occult power. Those who believe that hypnosis can be used to perform miracles or control minds are, of course, simply sharing the view of the consensus that ruled for centuries and which is still predominant. History is full of tempting scenes.

Mesmer was the first to suggest a rational basis for the effects of hypnosis. Although we now know that his notion of 'animal magnetism' has moved from a healer to a patient through a mysterious ethereal fluid, hopelessly misguided, it is firmly based on the scientific ideas at the time, especially the gravity theory of Isaac Newton. At that time, many tried to reach the secrets of alchemy, including Newton himself. He considered nothing less than the first matter, the sacred spirit of alchemy, *prima materia* – the essence in the heart of things or the spirit that permeates matter. The concept of the first matter is analysed by Jung, who analysed the psychological aspects of matter. He considers *prima materia* as an unknown substance that transmits the projection of autonomic mental content.

But let's return to the Western interpretation of hypnosis. Mesmer was the first to develop a consistent method of hypnosis, which was adopted and developed by his followers. It was a very ritual practice. Mesmer, for example, liked to perform mass induction by connecting his patients with a rope through which his 'animal magnetism' could pass.

Inevitably, these 'magical' traps brought Mesmer to ruin. Hypnosis is a complex process, not a little harmless, which has an impact on the hypnotherapist and can lead to confusion that can pass into paranoia. In practice, it turned out that a lot of people just happened by it. Nevertheless, the fact remains that hypnosis works, and in the nineteenth century, it is characterised by individuals who are searching for its meaning and applying its effects.

Surgeons and doctors such as John Elliotson and James Esdaille began to use hypnosis in the field of classical medicine, risking their reputations, and researchers such as James Braid, who began to delve into layers of mesmerism, revealing physical and biological truths at the core of the phenomenon, are going a step ahead of their colleagues. Thanks to their persistence and efforts, by the end of the century, hypnosis became accepted as a serious clinical technique, applied in large universities and hospitals.

This trend continued in the twentieth century, although in a way, hypnosis has become a method that has been pushed shyly into the other. Important changes were taking place elsewhere. First of all, the focus centre on the hypnotic method moved from Europe to America, where almost all the most significant breakthroughs in the science of the twentieth century occurred.

Second, hypnosis has become a popular phenomenon, something that has been increasingly available to laymen outside the laboratory or clinic. At the same time, the style of hypnosis has changed, from open applications carried out by people from authority to secret experiments that have been conducted on individuals or groups. Hypnosis of that time was carried out on the basis of keywords in a particular language. This is mainly the style of work of a therapist such as Milton H. Erickson.

More importantly, perhaps, hypnosis has become more and more a method that is being implemented in practice and is considered a useful tool to relieve psychological stress and lead to profound changes in different situations. This topic is very up to date. Progress in neurology, coupled with the work of British psychologists Joe Griffin and Ivan Tyrrell, who linked hypnosis with rapid eye movement, REM, also helped to resolve the debates, introducing hypnosis and hypnotic trance into the realm of everyday practice.

RTS: How would you, in short, say what the official history of hypnosis is so far?

GSF: The history of hypnosis is a search for something that is apparent to everyone present, a universal phenomenon that is an inseparable part of a human being.

RTS: And what would you say about the future of hypnosis?

RTS: The future of hypnosis will be fully realised through the incredible potential of our natural hypnotic abilities.

5

Ego

RTS: What role does ego play for man's activity, and what does he actually represent?

GSF: Ego is nothing more than a person's consciousness of himself. It is the information we have about ourselves. The ego is a sub-program of the main life-sustaining program that can, as such, encourage egocentric behaviour. Although, in principle, the ego is not at all negative as it is generally presented, too strong. The ego can cause focus primarily on its own needs regardless of the consequences for another person or the environment.

The ego functions exclusively in a conscious state. An actively egoistic person constantly shows his superiority, physical strength, financial power, or dominance in every sense. This program is extremely powerful and very often dominates the person's life. It is very convenient for manipulation in the system of rewards and confirmation, acceptance and approval. It increases in time with the individual as well as in the masses, which means that the ego, if not limited and not directed, can grow into a phenomenon we call egocentricity, its orientation primarily and often exclusively to our own needs or desires.

I would clarify this a little more because the ego is a very sensitive field that needs to be given maximum attention. The ego's injuries can have many consequences. Thus, a person under the dominance of the ego dedicates all his abilities, opportunities, and attention to satisfy his ego in every place and at any moment seek constant confirmation in himself or in his own environment. Each confirmation is an incentive for an egocentric and essential condition for increasing dominance over the environment in which one is located or with which one is confronted. Both are very important for the one whose ego is oversized. When the environment receives reactions in the form of admiration, praise, positive incentive, the person stimulates his ego even further and continues in that direction of 'upgrading'.

The egocentric person is characterised by 'blind' obedience, humility, and flattery towards the superiors so that after termination of contact with them, the complete domination of their ego can be demonstrated in their surroundings. It goes into the psychotic and aggressive states of an egocentric individual with a desire for complete domination. If such a person does not receive the appropriate feedback, anxiety, even a depressive state that can develop into a disease, occurs.

RTS: Can you give us some examples?

GSF: There are many examples, but I will give you some to get a better idea of what is actually the ego. Perhaps the most intelligible and the most typical examples of the strong ego and its constant stimulation are in royal families, politicians, famous actors, and public figures.

A special example of ego manipulation is in the military, where the ego incentive is carried out for the purpose of 'blind obedience' and execution of extreme tasks. For example, in Nazi Germany, Goebbels knew about the power of the ego, and with the propaganda machinery, he managed to lift the ego to the whole nation and persuade them that they were chosen, the best, the mightiest, and that they could do all. His 'success' is evident. So many millions of people blindly followed the instructions, perfectly obedient to go to war for the satisfaction of ego and victory. Nowadays, we have extremists who are subjected to brainwashing and parallel lifting of the ego, so they are able to endanger their own lives. Such people, after 'processing', thought that they were God's warriors, chosen.

The huge success of Facebook and social networks just lies in the fact that it is a huge field for the satisfaction of ego and exhibitionism, where people often and falsely represent satisfactory ego, satisfying their inner instincts. I said 'instincts' – and not by chance. The desire to be the best, the most beautiful, the most successful, etc. – that is, satisfying and feeding our own ego – emerged from the drive for self-sustaining, strengthening, and continuing life in a better or easier way. The urge for food or the satisfaction of other life needs is very close to the need to satisfy the ego, only the ego includes the sum of the needs of the individual concentrated in one focus – 'my needs are the most important!'

RTS: Is the development of egocentricity a positive or negative process?

GSF: Developing the egocentricity of a person can achieve remarkable success, but this success can never be permanent because it is based on constant confirmation, so when there is no permanent confirmation, it happens that they either lose what their ego feeds or enter into deep depression.

In my clinical practice, I had a large number of cases of people with depression that just came from the manipulation of the ego. But fortunately, this can be resolved with great success when a person stops identifying with his ego and stops asking for constant endorsements from his environment. To heal, to say so, comes from gaining self-confidence because the basis of egocentrism is that the person does not feel 'worthy' enough. This occurs as a result of the presence of subconscious thoughts that life is endangered in all situations and at any moment.

Religious fanatics, self-portraits, kamikaze fighters, and members of certain sects and organisations are manipulated by the ego system through a system of 'selected' and 'rewarded' new life in paradise where 'there is no death'. Egocentricity creates constant tension, nervousness, and even aggression in people, so there is a very thin line between an egocentric man and a psychopath. The psychopath is always an egocentric.

RTS: Can an individual draw the boundary between healthy ego strengthening and egocentrism?

GSF: For such a thing, first of all, a clear picture is needed – that is, the performance of an individual about himself and his environment. When I say a 'clear picture', first and foremost, the emotional state of a person is balanced. In many techniques, self-help and meditation insists on pushing the ego because the ego creates tension and neurosis, and it is difficult to find relaxation or a meditative state.

Most often, gurus, teachers, life guides, and mental trainers are not aware of the ego and its system of functioning, which leads to the complete confusion of followers and their entering into severe depressive states. They are equally convinced that meditations release the ego when, in fact, it is the completely opposite. As soon as the person finds himself in a situation that suits him, it will fully reintroduce his egocentricity. Egocentric people can be highly intelligent and very wisely masquerade their egocentricity only temporarily, while the so-called coaches, gurus, teachers, guides, and others think that by their techniques, they have eliminated the ego's influence. This short period can deceive both the individual and the persons who surround him.

Egocentric people are not aware of their condition. They are even convinced of the correctness of egocentric behaviour and action, thinking that the environment does not understand them, confirming the domination of their ego. A characteristic phenomenon is that given unprofitable positive feedback from the environment of an egocentric person, they express anger, hatred, sadness, and depression.

'Erasing the ego' is one of a number of examples of various misconceptions and practices that lead to the misconception and confusion of the followers, leaving them with the consequences of paranoid phobias. I would compare such an approach with the so-called psychological crushing of delicate or war prisoners. 'Slamming the psyche' by various psychological methods leads to a complete counter-effect.

RTS: What would be the spiritual definition of the ego?

GSF: From a spiritual perspective, the ego represents a state in which we consider ourselves separate from others and God because we have identified ourselves with the physical body and impressions in the various centres of the subtle body. In short, the ego guides our lives on the basis of the belief that our existence is limited by our five senses, mind, and intellect and identifying with them to a certain extent.

According to the spiritual science, our true state of existence is the identification with the soul or the principle of God in us and the maintenance of that consciousness in everyday life. As the same principle of God exists in all of us, from a spiritual perspective, in the creation of God, there is the unity of spirit and matter. However, depending on the level of the ego, to a different extent, we identify with God's principle, i.e. the soul. If our ego is high, we are less identified with the soul or with God's principle in us.

RTS: From the angle of a hypnotherapist, how do you explain the ego?

GSF: In the cyclical dictionary, the ego can be defined as pride in itself or the need to be better than we are. Thoughts like 'my body and mind', 'my intellect', 'my life', 'my wealth', 'my wife and children', 'I deserve to be happy', etc. come only from the ego.

Self-awareness, pride, ubiquity, and *jast* are words that are related to the word *ego* or *aham* but from a psychological angle. Fully and objectively confronting one's needs, environment, and desires lead to a healthy ego. Any deviation from this leads to a condition called ego-centeredness or an extremely opposite state of affairs – altruism or excessive concern for others at the very least.

Bringing in the balance of the notion of self and the world around us as well as the harmonisation of our needs with respect to the environment, we call emotional as well as spiritual harmony. A balanced ego is a consequence of this state. Any oscillation from this is a disorder that can cause deeper or greater disorders that affect the psychic and focal health of man.

RTS: How does the image of a man with an ego look like?

GSF: The following drawing, which is based on knowledge of the spiritual dimension, shows a person who has an ego. The drawing was drawn by the seeker of the Spiritual Knowledge Research Foundation, SKRF, with a developed sixth sense. A dark envelope that can be seen around the soul is an egoistic person. As the ego of this person is high, the person does not identify with the soul. Because of the person's eye, a black envelope is formed. When the ego is blocked, so is the flow of God's grace. The black energy, blocking access to divine grace, negatively influences the life of that person.

Mass is a similar case, which is an unrealistic fantasy with the stated consequences for those who follow it. I have had in my practice many such cases with the consequences of the above text, which have undeniably proved to me that these are fantasies that lead people to great misconceptions. I will cite examples of attitudes and findings of contemporary psychology and psychiatry associated with narcissism which are absolutely correct and explain the complexity and connection of characteristics. One of them and narcissism. I will briefly state the main features of the narcissistic personality disorder.

It has already been mentioned that a narcissistic personality disorder is only revealed in puberty. It is also important to say that today this is not considered a disease but primarily a condition. Thus, a narcissistic personality disorder is a personality that is initially badly formed, without a fully built identity and a firm foothold in itself or without self-confidence. This disorder is much more difficult to deal with than neurotic disorders. Therapy is long lasting and often does not end with complete success, but there is a possibility of tolerance of this disorder. Success is also considered when the patient partially regains his condition and begins to control and tolerate it.

In very rare cases, there is complete reparation of personality and the completion of all omissions in early development. The inner world of a person suffering from a narcissistic personality disorder is quite empty. These people build false images of themselves. In their early childhood, they did everything to 'buy' their mother's love and attention, in adulthood investing heavily in that false image to love others, not to be accepted and worshiped by other people.

These people always have the 'idea of size' – that is, the idea of being more beautiful, more successful, smarter than others. For them, the world is a mirror. They perceive only what fits into their false and grandiose image, while other aspects of reality are neglected. If no one admires them, they feel 'broken' and completely empty. False and superficial happiness is felt only when they have an audience, and they are very unwilling to tolerate loneliness. These people do not have authenticity. They are not 'original' because they have not managed to build their identity. They do not enjoy anything in their own way.

Narcissists strive for success not to have money but to achieve fame, to attract other people to admiration. Therefore, they are prone to various manipulations. They always tend to get the attention of those who are enjoying themselves, and when they manage to make them their 'subjects', they begin to despise them or, at the very least, to be completely disinterested in them.

These people do not have deep feelings. They are not able to love nor to hate. The feeling, very intense and vigorous, that they find in themselves to explode the moment they are stricken is anger. Narcissistic rage is explosive, very violent and strong, and arises at any disagreement of the wishes of Narcissus. The more important the desire that is shaken, the stronger the explosion of anger.

RTS: How can we recognise a person's narcissistic disorder?

GSF: The *Psychiatric Diagnostic Manual* lists the criteria by which we can recognise narcissistic personality disorder:

- A grandiose feeling of exaggerated importance
- Preoccupation with fantasies of unlimited success, power, beauty, or ideal love
- Belief that they are special and can only be understood by other special people or people of high status
- Requirement of excessive admiration
- Unreasonable expectations that one must receive a particularly good treatment or automatic agreement of others in view of their wishes
- Difficulty to exploit others to achieve their own goals
- Lack of faculty of compassion with others and reluctance to recognise the feelings and needs of others
- Tendency to seduce others or believe that others envy them
- Display of arrogant and sober behaviour and attitudes

People with narcissistic personality disorder usually come to therapy because of depression, squinting, a feeling of emptiness. With such people, it is not easy to do therapeutic work because they are very cunning, so they often oppose the authority of the therapist. Also, they are often addicted to drugs or alcohol or some kind of psychostimulant, which additionally makes it difficult to work with them. They use drugs or alcohol to complete this chronic lack of emotion, so they are very hard to give up.

It is especially difficult to establish a good working alliance with these people because they are unconcerned and inclined to think only about what they hear. Although they can be very intelligent, it is right to bring them closer to emotions and to tell them to really authentically live and work out their problems. For this reason, the treatment of these patients is often long and sometimes incomplete.

However, in a significant number of cases, a shift and improvement is generally achieved. Given that we have said that a narcissistic personality disorder is a state rather than a disease, these patients are not treated with medication but by a beneficial and accepting therapeutic relationship that serves as a substitute for a childbearing relationship from childhood.

6

Spiritism

RTS: What does spiritism mean for you, and where can you place it in the context of information and energy?

GSF: If we stick to the way spiritism is interpreted in Wikipedia, it is an occult science that seeks to establish communication with deceased people. The spiritism movement evolved in the nineteenth century, when Allan Kardec exposed his postulates in the *Book of Ghosts* (1858). He slowly transferred to Europe in that period from the American continent. However, the roots of spiritism, communication with deceased people, go far, much earlier in the history of human civilisation, and are not unique to one nation or located on one continent but across the globe.

Among the ancient African tribes, there was an entire ritual that was attached to a spirit that, after death, moved into a tree and is very honoured today among the indigenous tribes. Today there is a custom in the people to 'knock on the tree' to 'not hear evil'. The cult of the spirit that moves after death in some other form is also present in other old civilisations and on other continents, not only in Africa. And among the Slovene people, especially the Serbs, it was believed that the souls of the deceased settled in trees and plants. Allow me to quote Veselin Čaykanović, doctor of philosophy and PhD professor of philosophical faculties in Belgrade, who dealt with ethnology . . .

'When I said that certain trees – some specimens or whole species – belong to certain demons or deities, I have especially used this vague term. What is the affiliation, connection between the tree and the demon? There are scientists – for example, Otto Kern, a Hoole professor – who think that the tree or plant itself, as such, has never been worshiped but that its religious character and reputation come from where it could possibly be flat, temporary, or permanent, as well as what kind of deity or demon resides in it. Sacred wood, therefore, would be nothing more than the most primitive temples since the temples in paganism were indeed nothing but buildings in which the deity lives, in a certain contradiction with the present temple, which is primarily the chamber. Moreover, Pliny the Elder, from the first century after Christ, said of the wood that the "temples of the gods" were *numinum* temples. However, in our national religion, they existed, and there was one . . . understanding that the tree can be, first of all, shelter, the seat of the human soul. The proofs are fruit trees and wood that is planted by graves and in which people imagine the soul of the deceased. From folk literature and from folk beliefs, we know that from Momir's grave, the pine came out, and from Grozdanin's the vine, or from the grave of another guy the vine, and a girl's the rose, that the blood of the Kosovo heroes dyed the peony, and from the grave of St John Vladimir, the ivy emerged.'

The ancient Egyptians tried to establish contact with their dead, leaving them records in the form of certain signs. Where are your signs? Are these the first written evidence of the exchange of information? Etymologically, spiritism originates from the Latin word *spiritus*, 'spirit', and denotes communication with ghosts. Spiritism is, to put it simply, the belief in the existence of ghosts or that there are 'souls' of the dead from the 'other side' with which we can establish communication and information exchange directly or through the media.

The act is attributed by the church to occult, prohibited, and 'dirty' actions because 'the souls of the dead should rest in peace'. The question is whether the church explicitly recognises the existence of 'foreign human souls', regardless of the Holy Spirit. This vague dualism creates a lot of confusion and provides space for the manipulation of the gullible by the 'media' who claim to establish communication with the dead.

The modern history of spiritism began in 1848. The first documented event on supernormal phenomena happened after the Fox family moved into a house in the village of Hydeville in the state of New York. There is a whole description of this event. The case triggered the sensation, and the family, allegedly visiting and harassing ghosts, had to relocate to their relatives' residence in the nearby city of Rochester. However, the Fox family, according to their allegations, reported some strange events there, which attracted public attention on a large scale.

In the course of 1849, a series of sessions were held at the Fox house, where inexplicable phenomena were recorded, such as moving objects in the room, furniture levitation, and the like. The Fox family members took advantage of this self-promotion event and public practice of spiritualist sessions, prompted by those who had previously doubted the possibility of communicating with the dead.

Since then, there has been an increasing popularity of spiritualist sessions, which is for the infertile students to try to find a scientifically justified and rational explanation of these phenomena. That's right. Dr James Baird set up a theory in 1853 that implies that the tables were being triggered during a spiritualist session under the astonishment of the expectations of those who sat around them, while English physicist and chemist Michael Faraday argued that the movements that made the product grow were because of the hands of the present.

It's interesting to look at what the Bible says – 'Do not turn to those who call upon the spirits . . . that you do not become impure because of them' (Leviticus 19:31). The Bible clearly states God's attitude towards the invocation of ghosts. Although this practice was common in ancient times, the law given by God to the Israelites was as follows – 'Let no one find in you any spirits or ask for the dead. For whoever does such a thing is not in the grace of God' (Deuteronomy 18:10–12). The Bible also says that those who deal with any kind of occultism 'will not inherit the kingdom of God' (Galatians 5:19–21).

Further, the Bible says of the influence of the dead on the living, 'The living are conscious that they will die, but the dead are unaware of anything . . . and their love and their hatred and their jealousy [all that they felt while they were alive] disappeared' (Ecclesiastes 9:5, 6). So the Bible teaches that the dead are simply dead. They cannot think or do anything, so they do not serve God either. 'The dead do not praise [God], nor do any of those who descend in silence' (Psalms 115:17). 'Is it [the man] turning to the dead for life?' (Isaiah 8:19).

Chapter 28 of the first Book of Samuel speaks of the unfaithful king Saul, who violated God's command not to turn to those who call upon ghosts. He went to a woman who allegedly communicated with the dead, specifically God's servant, Samuel. But was that really Samuel? No. She talked to someone who pretended to be a dead Samuel. It was an evil spirit that served the 'father of lies', Satan (John 8:44). Why do these evil spirits – that is, the demons – represent the view that the dead continue to live? They want to oppose God and downplay his Word, the Bible (2 Timothy 3:16).

The question is, does this then mean that according to what the Bible claims for the dead, there is no hope? Of course not. The Bible speaks of the future resurrection of the dead, when all those who sleep in the grave will rise up (John 11:11–13, Acts 24:15). Until then, we can be sure that those who have died do not experience any suffering. From all of the above, it can be concluded that the Christian religion, at the same time, promotes the existence of the soul and prohibits – that is, satanises – communication with the souls of the dead. There is a huge field for manipulation, which I would especially talk about and what I have managed to prove.

RTS: Can one speak of a person's, let us call it, innate instinct to believe in ghosts, i.e. spiritism?

GSF: You see, it's quite understandable that those who lose a beloved person want to make sure that she does not suffer anywhere and that 'although she left the earthly world', they can continue to communicate with her. So perhaps, they think, 'Why don't we go to someone who invites ghosts? Perhaps that would calm us down.'

Many claim that the dead, in a way, continue to live. Therefore, they try to contact them, perhaps to get some information from them or to make them smarter so that they no longer harass the living. The desire of man for 'eternal life' is as strong as the urge to maintain the species, hence the great desire to establish contact with the deceased, i.e. with their spirit.

RTS: How do you interpret the fact that the spiritualist medium sometimes presents incredible details?

GSF: It is very common that those who attended spiritualist sessions claim that those who invoke ghosts reveal information that only the deceased could have known as well as his family or close friends. The medium is the main personality and leads the session. The success of communication with the deceased depends on him. There are different ways of communicating with the dead, but everything is based on the information exchange that forms the plasma, the figure, or the contours of the one with whom we 'communicate' in the form of memory nano-particles.

Here, I shall quote again Tesla, who said, 'Remember, no man who existed has died. He has turned into light and, as such, exists and continues. The secret is that these light particles return to their original state.' Nikola Tesla was convinced that no man and no living being who had died had disappeared forever. 'Life has an infinite number of forms, and the duty of a scientist is to find it in every form of matter. At first, there was energy and then matter, which was created from the original and eternal energy we know as light. It was shining, and the stars, planets, man, and everything on Earth and in the universe appeared.'

In the bodies of living beings, he noticed the same characteristics in the case of technical devices like the radio. On the basis of Ososnov, he would have come to the conclusion that our bodies are, at the same time, the receivers and transmitters of energy, of life. 'The whole life of a man is just an electric current,' Tesla claimed, 'and his mind is light.' If a radio device was broken, the man from the previous two centuries would have thought with certainty that the cell that the receiver caught disappeared, which, of course, is not true in practice. The station still exists. However, the receiver can no longer catch it. According to Tesla's claims, so is this with the bodies of living beings.

Our bodies are the receivers of life or energy that will not disappear with death. 'There is a core in the universe from where we get all the strength, all the inspiration. It attracts us forever. I feel its power and values that it broadcasts throughout the universe and thus keeps it in line. I did not break into the secret of this core, but I know it exists. There are life energies in every corner of the universe. One of them is immortality, whose origin is beyond man and is awaiting him,' Tesla said.

Wherever there is a form of life, there must also be a soul, 'the soul is life', whether it is an amoeba or a human being. It is present within each body. The soul represents energy – that is, the force activated by everyone's body that enables it to function, the driven electric current that creates voltage when passing through the copper wire.

Throughout his life, man has several different bodies – those of the baby, the child, the young man, the middle-aged man, the old man.

However, all this time, in spite of physical transformation, we always retain the same characteristics with changing behaviour – that is, the reflection of our 'inner state'. So the question arises on whether we are material, the form of life in which the soul lives, which, after the death of the body, transforms into another form that represents energy or life.

RTS: What, in fact, is the process of communicating with the dead?

GSF: Energy or light particles that represent the essence of life and all of life, as well as communication processes, remain in old houses, old spaces, and this is the reason for the very frequent appearance of 'ghosts'. It is a very common case that the 'spirit of the dead' is recorded in the photographs of the living. Often the souls of the dead are not visible to the naked eye. However, they are often recorded with cameras. These unexplained phenomena of the appearance of grouped light particles as human faces before the death of the body still occupy my attention, and I have intensively explored this phenomenon.

The very process of communication or the exchange of information with the dead takes place through orb particles. There is an information field about which I had already spoken and clarified. I would just note that orb particles do not change state, nor can they be destroyed, because they represent energy that is indestructible.

During spiritualist sessions, there is often a tremor of the substrate or table on which they are leaning, hands placed on the downstream medium who establishes communication with the dead. I have on this issue one possible explanation, and it is based on the O-ring method, which is used today in quantum medicine, based on the resonance of electromagnetic waves, a phenomenon discovered by Mihailo Pupin. Dr Yoshiaki Omura applied the resonance phenomenon for diagnostic purposes, with scientifically proven justification of the application, and introduced the O-ring method in medical practice.

According to a similar principle, the process of establishing contact by the medium, who holds the hands of those present, is a firm backbone during the spiritistic session. The system for starting the object or vibrating the substrate or table is based on the principle of microwave vibrations that we produce, and we are not aware of them. And all this happens during the transmission of energy in the information field – that is, the establishment of receiving and sending information.

RTS: You have explored in detail spiritism or communication with the souls of the dead and the exchange of information with those who have left their material bodies to prove that it works. To what extent is the abuse of spiritism present today, and how can it be dangerous?

GSF: The most famous spiritualist session in the world is that in Medjugorje, which I witnessed in 1984. In the eighties, I dealt with scenic hypnosis. I had performances on stage scenes. I gained experience and popularity all over the former Yugoslavia. Namely, in the 1980s, the public claimed that in Medjugorje, a village near Citluk, some children had seen and had contact with Devica Marija, i.e. Gospo. Then, for a Communist environment, it was quite a surprise that something so freely spread to the public.

Things began to spread so quickly through the media, and soon, they began to talk about it in all parts of Yugoslavia. Opinions were divided between it being a scam and it being 'God's miracle'. The state ignored everything first, thinking that it would pass like any other sensation. However, as time passed, the whole thing was caught by *maha*. The Masonians formed a group that questioned it. State authorities arrested a chief priest and two others, all in all three associates. The chief priest who was arrested in Mostar was Fratar Zovko, which caused more attention.

The place of 'vision' was further visited. Fratar Zovko contacted his colleagues from the studios to organise a trip. His students were chief priests in places in Croatia, and they had organised a 'religious tour'.

The event was spread greatly, and masses of people began to come independently, especially the sick for healing. The phenomenon itself had caused interest among incurable patients. Namely, five children had had 'communication with the lady' at a certain time, seeing her. Fratar Zovko gave them the name *vidioci*. Otherwise, the narrow specialty of the friar during the studies was the psychology of religion, which I later learned. The sensational story of the appearance of the lady was so popular that people began to come, and control of the massive arrivals was gradually lost. The militia, which maintained order and led the 'pilgrims', could no longer maintain control over such a flow of people.

The Sarajevo newspaper *As* was one of the most dynamic and popular newspapers in the territory of Yugoslavia that had previously written about my performances, so I knew one of the editors personally. Once, sitting, he asked me what I had meant about the Lady in Medjugorje. I told him that I would invite the lady to the stadiums. In fact, I assumed it was a pure hypnosis, suggesting what others would want to see. I assumed that it was something like that. The editor wanted to write about it. He gave me a whole team of photographers and journalists to follow me to make a better and more complete story about the phenomenon in Medjugorje. He even gave me a journalistic ID for visiting Medjugorje to find out more.

When we appeared, I wanted to be introduced to Zovko, but around him, there was a mass of priests who did not allow direct contact with him without his permission, and at the same time, they helped the powerful people who came there. Fratar Zovko isolated children who supposedly saw the lady and did not allow any contact with them without his permission. As I presented myself as a journalist, at first, he was rather reserved, but when I told him we wanted a serious story, after the third day, I managed to talk to him. I was interested in the direct process of the session, not the visitors' stories. I wanted to see what it was about. Although Zovko was reserved, I managed to persuade him to be present at a couple of sessions, to take this picture, convinced him that this would be a serious phenomenon.

They had sessions at 18:45, 17:45 during the winter months. Why always at the same time? That was the first time I had ever seen such a thing, as if the lady had dictated to the children, 'Tomorrow I will appear at this time.' That in itself was an absurdity but, at the same time, a clear direction to what it really was. The session was timed, without exception. So he accepted that a photojournalist and I would be present at the 'sight' in a room near the church organised for this, receiving a hundred people. The children came here, but there were also people who paid for their cure for the children praying to the lady. These people were believers who did not doubt the appearance of the lady.

The friar Zovko, his assistants, the children, and numerous people were present. The children, on their knees, with their hands clasped, began to pray at six o'clock so that after forty-five minutes, there would be a 'sight'. After forty-five minutes, they were introduced to determine the state with the help of a set of prayers, along with others present. In a precisely timed manner, the children opened their eyes to whisper, as if they were talking to someone. It was interesting that they had open eyes. The session lasted for twelve to fifteen minutes, according to the orders of people who had paid for healing.

Fratar Zovko did not allow us to photograph the children in that state. Standing on their left, he had control, and occasionally, he suggested that the children ask for a particular person, for a particular family member, and so on. These were the individuals and families who came to worship the lady and pray for health.

When the session ended, the children would give a report on what was seen and heard and what the message transmitted to the lady was. I immediately saw that they had seen her differently, in different forms, clothes. Each one was different, which immediately told me that it was not about the object but about the 'impurities' on the side. The other thing was the various messages they had received 'for humanity' – peace, love, going to church. I got all the recorders and later analysed very carefully all those statements, which differed significantly.

I immediately understood what this was about – post-mortem suggestion, given, with variants of additives, depending on the 'order'. Some came to pray to the lord for health, some to give them a child, some for welfare, and the like. There, I spent fifteen days in the first round, establishing better contact with the priests and the friar Zovko, representing myself as a curious, 'stupid', and blind listener, trying to get as much information as possible to analyse everything better.

By exploring the whole thing, I came to the conclusion that the Franciscan Zovko, as soon as he finished college in Visoko, had gone to the army. After serving his military service, as a priest, he was sent to Medjugorje, where he had no more than twenty believers. He held the monastery with two nuns. But it was evident that Zovko was very intelligent, and his education – the philosophy and psychology of Catholicism – gave him the opportunity to teach children. Since he did not provide monastic life too much, to gain believers, he organised that, from Medjugorje and the surrounding villages, people bring children to the monastery as a kindergarten, where they would be guarded by nuns. He was doing it well and educating children in a free school. This was a significant form of help for parents who were mainly engaged in agriculture, growing tobacco and grapes. The children spent all day praying and singing religious songs. These were mostly children up to 7 years of age, in whom one could easily encode codes of conduct. So he had the ideal conditions to prepare the children for 'seeing'. I was sure it was suggestive manifestation in children. They had really experienced the Gospel, but they were programmed, targeted.

We made a series with eight extensions. The editor then was Džavid Husić. He prepared a great sensational story and even consulted the minister for religious communities that he would not be criticised by the state and would not lose credibility among the public. The Vatican had already complained about the arrest of a priest, and the

Communists did not want to argue with the Vatican. They forbade the release of Felton because it was the most painful. Felton stayed in the archives.

The matter in Medjugorje escalated. There was an expansion of religious tourism – from all over the world came the believers – pilgrimages to Medjugorje. This becomes a daily business worth millions. We left the story aside because the editor estimated that it should be so. However, the circle of people spread the story that I had perceived myself as deceived in Medjugorje but did not allow me to publicly declare it. After several years, I was contacted by an editor who had asked me for a story with a proposal to publish the story 'Offering Medjugorje' in two sequels.

The pope reacted and supported this story with his reaction. The pope then banned the participation of the Catholic Church in these sessions. He forbade the priests to have anything to do with it. My claim was that it was a spiritualist session mixed with post-hypnotic suggestion by invoking the dead – Mary, the mother of God – and that the Catholic Church strictly defended the conversations with the dead and with the demonic forces. The Catholic Church never wanted to officially acknowledge 'reporting to the Lady in Medjugorje', sending from time to time various commissions to examine the matter. In his statement to the public, Pope Francis voiced serious doubts about the indication of the Lady in Medjugorje, reluctantly claiming that there can be no word about Jesus's mother.

Those who 'saw the lady' propagated peace and love, and war occurred in those areas. As soon as the war broke out, the lady disappeared, but the monastery had earned a lot of money by then. Many reacted negatively to my intervals. They did not want me to spread the truth at the expense of their deception. I argued then – and even today I remain in that opinion – that it is about the sessions of appealing to the dead, spiritism, which it is explicitly against the Catholic Church, the Gospel of Luke, and even the entire Christian community.

This is a classic example of the popularisation of spiritism and manipulation. Money was not used by the friars to treat people, help people, but for their own enrichment as it did not bear fruit and appeal for peace and love. The war came, unfortunately. Medjugorje remained a place of prayer, which it should be, not a place of manipulation.

7

Telepathy

RTS: The transfer of thoughts among people is known in general as telepathy. What is your knowledge of this phenomenon as the ability to exchange thoughts across distances, and how do you explain this?

GSF: The term *telepathy*, as it is well known, originates from the Greek words *tele*, 'distant' and *pathe*, 'sense'. French researcher Friedrich Majers first used the word *telepathy* in 1882 at a gathering of a society for parapsychological research, with the explanation that it best describes the phenomenon that, until then, was referred to as 'reading thoughts'. His definition of telepathy is that 'the transfer of thought is independent of the recognisable channels of sensory perception'.

I define telepathy as 'the transmission of information between two or more subjects through decrypted channelling and information flows, without the use of common means of mutual communication'. A number of psychologists and psychiatrists and doctors have noted the special ability of telepathic communication in their patients, among them Sigmund Freud. He believed that telepathy was an ancient ability which was suppressed by evolution and could occur only under certain conditions.

On the contrary, Karl Jung, a well-known psychiatrist at the beginning of the twentieth century, felt that this phenomenon has a prominent role in human communication. The results of some studies show the accuracy of Jung's theory on the importance of telepathy. Because of the results of testing Jung's research, I am a follower of Jung's theory. Jung has even presented the theory by which societies function and are harmonised in their work precisely thanks to telepathy, which I fully agree with.

RTS: Have you had specific experiences in your practice that are related to this yet by enough unclear ways of communication among people?

GSF: Telepathy is among the first psycho phenomena which have become the subject of scientific research. The initial tests were very simple. For example, the sender would try to send the recipient information about a two-digit number, and the sender would be in one room and the recipient in another, which means that they are isolated in separate rooms. French philosopher Charles Ritch also introduced static probability, which made these scientific studies comparable. Research has shown that telepathy most often occurs in stressful and special situations among close friends and relatives.

Usually, telepathy was manifested by one person being aware of the dangers of the other person, seeing in the vision some parts of an event that had not yet happened. The person who sees this conveys his thoughts to the person in danger afterwards, and such information can influence the change of events. In folk traditions, this kind of telepathy is called premonition, and in psychological research, such cases of telepathy are the most common.

The people have the saying 'We are about a wolf – and a wolf at the door', which refers to the arrival of the person who was currently talking without the prior announcement of the arrival of the said person. The person is not sure whether we are at home at all and how we will respond to their arrival – to be happy, unpleasantly surprised, etc. This person sends his thoughts as information about himself, and at that moment, we begin to talk about them. The man is, at that moment, speaking at the door, which the people mentioned in the saying 'We are about a wolf – and a wolf on the door'.

According to researchers, telepathy is closely linked to the emotional state of the person. Women in these cases are more frequent 'users' of telepathy compared to men, which psychologists associate with their higher sensitivity and the fact that women are more reliant in terms of intuition than men. We will notice in everyday life that women have more respect for intuition and more sensibility than men. The most terrible telepathic communication occurs among the elderly.

Recent research has shown that some physiological elements in the human organism are also changing during telepathic experiences. There is an increase in the production of red blood cells and changes in the brainwaves of the recipient. Some drugs can stimulate telepathic abilities, which is interpreted by the action in their nervous system. Namely, their use increases the production of adrenaline in the body, which affects the telepathic ability of the individual.

From my experience, it has been narrated that people who use narcotic drugs to come to certain telepathic conditions are important persons – dealers, friends – and very strongly, they often confirm that this type of subconscious telecommunication functions. It turns out that the most expressive form of subconscious telecommunication is when a person is in a life-threatening situation.

I would also mention Rajhan's experiments, which represent significant research in this field. Namely, in the field of telepathy, one of the most important studies was carried out by Jozef Banks Rajhan, an American professor at Duke University, and his wife, Luiza. They started their experiments in 1927. They were trained with special maps, named after their assistant, Karl Zener, as Zener cards. Different symbols were printed on the maps – a five-pointed star, a circle, a square, a cross, and three wavy lines. Twenty-five such charts would be divided into five rows. In addition, a sender would sit alongside them and watch one of the cards persistently. In the other room, the receiver would show a symbol that, in his opinion, the sender sent.

Under the law of coincidence, by ordinary negotiation, an average of five to twenty possible hits can be achieved. So if the respondent hit five out of twenty-five maps, this was considered to be purely accidental. Some respondents had accurately hit eighteen cards, and Rajhan and his associates explained this as them having parapsychological abilities, telepathic abilities, and telepathic communication. The most successful among the 'telepaths' was one student who, in relation to other respondents, identified more often each card and, in a large number of cases, far more than other respondents.

These are the first attempts to come to the sharp condemnation of the scientific public. Indeed, Rajhan did not provide a statistically well-grounded explanation, causing doubt among a number of mathematicians as well as scientists who had carried out the experiments in laboratory conditions. In such research, it is impossible to test subjects under the same circumstances, which is a prerequisite for the scientific foundation of a study. Namely, since the basic assumption of parapsychology is that all phenomena are related to the personal experience of the respondents, two different persons will experience the same laboratory space differently, and therefore, the results become incomparable.

Lately, computers and computer games are increasingly used for such tests, and the respondent tries to guess which map the computer will show as the next one. Although many are sceptical of Rajhan's experiments, regardless of the narrow spectrum of conclusions and successfully proven hypotheses, these studies have indicated that 'something is happening' in this field because the obtained results deviate from the theory of probability and statistical results. Also, it should be kept in mind that these tests were performed in laboratory conditions – that is, experiments that were performed with constraints that are not quite ideal for obtaining adequate results. But they certainly make for important research that opened the door for others to explore this field. Some subsequent studies have resulted in less ambiguous results on telepathy, experimenting with pictures, maps, etc., but also about the influence of motivation on the effectiveness of telepathy.

In the middle of the last century, a number of studies were carried out with the support of the states. Specifically, in my practice, I noticed that with people who have access to certain information – that is, the 'key for deciphering the sending and receiving of information' using controlled channels at a higher level of awareness – they open up the possibility for mutual communication that we call telepathy. This does not apply to telepathic communication among people who are interconnected with powerful emotions but about people who have little or no knowledge of one another.

I have not experimented on this field too much because such kind of research, to be of good quality, should have wider and even official support. What this does not mean is that in the near future, I will not conduct more research on this. I would note that the biggest 'theft' of information occurs when the doctor establishes a diagnosis for a patient who will not tell him in case of severe, malignant diseases. It is very common that a patient, in an effort to discover the truth about his condition, 'reads' the diagnosis found by the doctor, and without insight into what he wrote or said, he already has in his thoughts the process in the form of information. This happens in altered states of consciousness.

Also, in twins, between the mother and the child, the fallen pairs come to this kind of communication as well as in specific situations in which an individual can be found. A man, in an effort to find out about someone or something, can establish a telepathic relationship with another person. So often we can hear from some people who are trying to find out what others think at a certain moment, 'I read it.'

The golden age in telepathy research begins in the 1960s, when world scientists were simply starting to race for who would get better results as soon as possible and 'control' these processes – that is, put them into use for certain purposes. It is well known that in 1966, on the relation of Novosibirsk–Moscow, telepathic communication was established by actor Karl Nikolaev and biophysicist Yuri Kamenski at a distance of nearly three thousand kilometres. Both, seen by scientific teams, were supposed to establish telepathic communication. Kamenski got a sealed package, randomly picked from the crowd of identical boxes, and after opening it, he had the task of merely replicating it. In Novosibirsk at the time, Nikolai should have recorded what Kamenski had thought at that moment, who closed his eyes with a metal spring made up of seven types of twisted spirals. Kamenski wrote, 'round, metal, shiny, toothed, resembling winding'. A few moments after that, Nikolaev wrote, 'long and thin, metal, black plastic'. After these impressive results, permission and funds for further research in this field were obtained by Russian officials.

Soon thereafter, the Popov group – bio-information sections of the scientific and technical association for radio engineering and electrical communications – by A. S. Popov were formed. The main task of this group of scientists was to discover the way in which telepathy takes place. For this research, special apparatuses were made, in addition to the EEG apparatus, which was used as a measuring instrument for certain brain reactions. These studies have largely led to telepathy and alpha rhythm, but this also affects other specific psychological conditions in which psychosis occurs, for example.

RTS: Another phenomenon closely related to the exchange of thoughts, i.e. the information you say, is psychosis. Would you like to say something about this on this occasion?

GSF: Let's start from the beginning by some method when we clarify things or phenomena. Psychokinesis originates from the Greek words *psycho*, 'spirit, life, soul', and *kinesis*, 'move'. The very phenomena of psychosis – or, as it is called, telekinesis – has been recorded in almost all parts of the world, even in ancient civilisations. The most famous telekinetics were D. D. Home, known for the ability of invisibility, Rudi Schneider, who could materialise and move objects, as well as, lately, Sai Baba.

Since the end of the 1930s, psychosis has become the most explored area of parapsychology, especially in the United States and the former USSR. Although many scientists have studied this phenomenon, the evidence still remains only superficial or hidden because the research is carried out by various secret institutions, i.e. the army, so that the results could later be used for military purposes. The biggest criticism of these studies is that they are not systematically monitored and do not have statistical confirmation.

I'll go back to Rajhan. Rajhan experimented in his laboratory on psychosis as well as telepathy, testing his ability to throw out dice. When throwing two simple dice, each subject should say beforehand which numbers on the dice will appear. The downside of this is that in this experiment, there is a simple statistical legitimacy, the possibility of a strike. Rajhan has arbitrarily determined the boundary on which the goal ceases to be pure luck or becomes a reading, proving the ability to negotiate. Unfortunately, the border was not statistically justified, and this experiment was publicly condemned.

In 1965, Rajhan founded his own institute for the exploration of the nature of man. Since that time, parapsychology has started to emerge significantly at colleges and in scientific circles. Rajhan immediately published his results for several reasons. The psychoanalyst was quite notorious at the time, 1934, had no objections of objectivity, and could not control the conditions of his experiments. When he finally published them, Rajhan argued in his paper that psychosis has nothing to do with brain activity or with the usual laws of mechanics. Rather, it is an immaterial force that overcomes matter and cannot be measured or explained by physicists. In this work, Rajhan linked telepathy and psychosis, arguing that telepathy is a necessary part of psychosis that must, at a precise moment, be included in the movement of the object.

As we know, they were not the only ones. The escalation of such research begins sometime in 1945. Psychokinesis is divided into macro and micro psychosis, i.e. visible and invisible results. At the end of 1960, Helmut Schmidt devised a way to measure micro psychokinetic influences. He constructed a special coin-throwing device and asked the respondents to predict the results of the throw. This device is the forerunner of random number generators that were later used in the computer industry. Schmitt experimented also with the psychokinetic abilities of animals, and today similar methods are used in similar experiments.

Among the most famous macro psychokinetic events was the so-called Geller effect. For the first time, Geller discovered his telekinetic ability by using the clock which his stepfather had given him when he went to school. While he watched him intently, one day he noticed that the hands moved faster. At the age of 13, Uri began to master his powers. For example, by concentrating, he could read the thoughts of worthy students when they wrote school assignments. In time, he decided to cash in on his ability, and in 1972, he started on a tour of Germany. He participated in a series of television shows and impressed the viewers with his ability to bend metal, acting on the metal with his mental abilities. Geller's powers seemed to be such that some viewers claimed for him to have modified furniture in their homes that were far from a television studio. However, Geller could not repeat his performance in laboratory conditions.

In spite of the fact that individuals cannot fully demonstrate their psychokinetic abilities in laboratory conditions because in some way, they encroach on closed spaces, many good results of psychokinetic research have emerged from laboratory conditions. The state of 'general nonsense', 'concentrated passivity', and 'relaxed attention' as one type of concentration required for people with telepathic or psychokinetic abilities, is achieved equally well in laboratory and 'home' conditions. However, the occurrence of these phenomena is still rare and considered abnormal, something that causes a lot of curiosity and even provokes fear from people with specific psychokinetic abilities.

The Russians uncovered their most famous psychokinetic to the world and the public in 1968. Nina Kulagina, a housewife from then Leningrad, today St Petersburg, showed that she could move items of different sizes and shapes, change the direction of the movement of objects already in motion, and leave fingerprints. Although the psycho-science is not recognised by scholars, it is considered that the experiments conducted in strictly controlled conditions have made this part of parapsychology the closest science.

Nikolai Aleksandrovich Kozyrev was a Russian astronomer and astrophysicist whose work contrasted with the knowledge of official science at the time, so he remained unrecognisable and, in some way, forgotten. Russian scientists did not know how to apply themselves to the famous patented Kozyrev mirrors, which were used to see miraculous phenomena. These mirrors, such as lenses, focus on different types of radiation. The experiments of Nikolai Kozyrev have been tested many times, and every time, their results are confirmed.

After Koryrev's death, experiments with the mirrors were carried out at the institute for experimental medicine. By moving inside the mirror, people were able to emit distant thoughts, see images from the future and the past, even events that went beyond reality. In 1997, Nino-Siberian scientists conducted experiments together with English colleagues in England at Stonehenge. More than two hundred people participated in the experiment. Primaries were sent via Kozyrev's mirrors from Novosibirsk. The scientists were convinced that the mirrors functioned. The results were ten times greater than the percentage of chance.

There were other experiments in the field of telepathy which were done by Morse alphabet. One of the great successes in the field of telepathy research was achieved in the USSR in the 1980s. Then, for the first time with measuring instruments, irrefutable evidence of establishing a mental telepathic communications was found. For the experiments, the biophysicist Kamenski travelled to Novosibirsk, a city 3,200 kilometres away from Moscow. On this occasion, the aforementioned Moscow actor and journalist Nikolaev, who was in Moscow, was connected with an encephalograph, which records brain impulses. As soon as Kamenski began to send pictures of the maps, the brain pulses of Nikolaev began to change. They were different from normal impulses, i.e. in the normal state. Nikolic's mapping of the cards went very well, but they soon realised that the same brain irritations could also be created while Kamenski imagined to fight with Nikolaev. Kamenski could transmit points and lines of the Morse alphabet by imagining battles of different durations. Forty seconds of imaginary fighting produced a sample of brain pulses read as a dash, while a fifteen-minute battle represented a point. In this way, the students in Moscow could decipher, for example, the Russian word *mig*, a wink – a moment that telepathic Morse was sent to Kamenski from Siberia from a distance of 3,200 kilometres.

The previous knowledge I have shown that the Russians were the most valuable in the field of experiments and especially in the study of telepathy – the Novosibirsk Institute for Clinical and Experimental Medicine, which examined telepathy across a long distance – had been convened. the territorial distance absolutely does not play a role in the process of telepathy. The phenomenon of telepathy means that communication between two figures happens subconsciously. Jung said – and I absolutely agree with it – that communication happens all the time, but it is subconscious. This communication is either with someone or with the environment or is a global plan. If telepathy is engaged as a global plan, it follows that there is communication among a mass of people.

I responsibly claim that our brain is, at the same time, a 'receiver' and a 'transmitter' of information and that the information transfer between people takes place on the unique principle of channelling and decoding this information. These are processes that can happen in a conscious state, but in our subconscious, they generate information that has a certain meaning and can be 'triggers' for various things, both positive and negative.

RTS: When telepathy is concerned, are there people born with this 'mechanism'?

GSF: The most conclusive and most suitable for interrogation is communication that takes place between two people. Namely, the tests have shown that unidirectional twins have the best results of telepathic communication. The question that arises is why this is so? Because the uniquely twinned wavelengths and vibrations are very similar.

Communication, such as mobile phone communication, requires a certain connection and a switchboard that will connect the participants. It should not be considered technically or physically at all because it is a method of mental communication that does not have cables or wires, nor does it take place through a device. For comparison, when we observe telepathy between two hands as a connection between two phones – one is in Australia and the other in Serbia – it is necessary that the caller knows the number, and the call goes over the central or satellite. The satellite sends a signal to the recipient's phone, and the phone rings.

If we compare this system with mental communication, we can come to the conclusion that we are sending information to the cosmos and around ourselves. Somewhere in the cosmos, this cosmic switch connects the one that is called, gives them a signal, and the receiver seizes it. In each one of us, there is a premonition of telepathic connection, only we recognise it very rarely or only in extreme cases. A man is inclined to do so, and he hides it in himself – that is, he denies his abilities. The well-known phenomenon of single-minded twins is that if one hurts their leg, no matter what point on the planet, the other twin will feel the same pain. So we can say that this is a mental teleportation of information.

Professor of quantum physics Vlatko Vedral has already worked with his team on the teleportation of nano-particles. They are currently in the process of proving that the teleportation of information is possible and is happening. Therefore, we can define telepathic communication as the teleportation of information. Since we are blocked from consciously reading this information, it goes away and is stored in our memory as a particular file and remains there as information.

RTS: Can telepathic communication be established with all people, and is it unique to a person?

GSF: It often happens that a person suddenly changes his mood, that he is concerned with anxiety, depression, etc. One of these cases is recognised when a mother who is waiting for her child says she is not sure that something is wrong with the child, and later, she would find out that the child has a problem. Then the manifestation of telepathy occurs in the human environment and without man's conscious influence. This process takes place between him and the plants, between him and the animals.

From high school, you will get all the benefits and intentions of the work as well as animals and plants. The experiment is a testimonial of human beings. Telepathy is evidently present. It was, is, and will be among all living beings. In addition, it should be accompanied by the installation and systematisation of information and their transmission.

The phenomenon of the epithelium is that of a man, alive, and the living, and he works in the same way as a woman in the phenomenon of cell medicine. How frequent, how it is established and manifests itself through the behaviour of animals, and how these interactive relationships between man and plants, man and animals, plants and animals are taking place is still at the stage of intensive research, and many attempt to put this phenomenon under as much light as possible.

This evidently exists, i.e. it takes place through the cosmic processes of the bio-information field, but the mechanisms of willing activation and deactivation have not yet been investigated. I believe that all these answers are waiting for you, and will be given to the Creator's thoughts. This is scientifically affirmed at the same time as the method of communicating with a patient, intersection of the phenomenon of an epithelium from an animal to a man. For now, there is evidence that he is a one-way gentleman, able to tolerate life, alignment. I'm not quite sure about that.

Scientific experiments show that this disables information from telepathic self-reliance. Man has the ability to communicate with a variety of lifelike words in a patient's language. The mood of a patient can be traced back to a woman in the same class, as if she was a victim of any kind of communication. She had a lot of, like those of mammals, attributes which are more pronounced.

We know the phenomenon of intercourse. It makes an announcement of the situation, for example, human contact or telepathic contact of the transmission of a person's lover. We will flood it with 'Today we like to think like . . .' The trainer will be able to use the handset for certain performances. It is due to the fact that some of the younger people have been able to achieve better results during the first half of the year, and this time, they will return to the previous story.

Numerous, very often unnoticed, cases are part of our everyday life, which undoubtedly shows that telepathy works but, as we have already said, without our knowledge but in the subconscious as a signal and certain preoccupation. Our mood, which is suddenly changing, can influence telepathic communication. If it sucks in a strong love affair and constantly subscribes to a beloved person, its characteristic lines, in their own way, can cause positive feelings with a loved one. For example, quizzes have shown that for people who really like each other, telepathic communication is more pronounced and achieves better results than people who do not like or do not even know each other.

Jung's assumptions and claims regarding telepathic communication are completely correct, and the results of my analysis speak in favour of it. Telepathy is happening to people when they are in direct physical contact or if they are not in physical contact at all but have, say, a desire for communication. What I would mention in particular – and I consider it extremely important – is the telepathic communication between the doctor and the patient.

A patient visiting the doctor comes up with a desire to find out whether there is a solution for him or not. That is why he is wondering whether the doctor will help or not. In terms of the appearance, attitude, behaviour, and speech of the physician, the patient consciously tries to come to a conclusion for the problem and subconsciously, including the telepathic communication system, attempts to steal information as to what kind of doctor the results actually came from.

Some experiments showed that doctors who were confident in therapy and healing in relation to the patient had much more success than doctors who suspected diagnosis and therapy as the right cure but also the patient's telepathic ability to 'tame' this information. These processes, which are performed in the subconscious, are known to neither the doctor nor the patient, but this also affects the outcome of the treatment to a certain extent.

My conclusion, confirmed by the research, is that telepathy is, in fact, a method teleportation of information which is also confirmed not to be known so far, but it is a special newly discovered energy that has the capabilities of teleportation. By activating this type of energy, we establish a process called telepathy. Man's 'censorship and autonomy' of the mind is a membrane that stops, in my opinion, a completely natural process of information exchange.

8

Significance — Truth or Obligation

RTS: Can you tell us, in principle, what do you think about the psychic?

GSF: Remember, only the Creator knows the future. The human species, in its thought process, only speculates, predicts, suggests. You see, I would not completely like to exclude the fact that there really are people who are able to receive certain information about other people or phenomena. Of course, this is a limited scope. When I say 'limited scope', I mean, first of all, the type and amount of information. It is not for a human alone to know everything about the events that are coming. These 'abilities' or attributes can be attributed only to the Creator.

Despite the fact that there are suspicions that a person is able to access information through a channel of communication and certain codes, this phenomenon has so far been manipulated by various 'psychics' who, in essence, for the sake of popularity and the acquisition of material resources, have been deceiving people through history, and even today they are cheating the entire public. But I will try to explain in an extremely rational and pragmatic manner this ability – that is, the specific way of receiving information that is specific to the individual.

Since there is human civilisation, it is known that in various religions, movements, and groups, people are propounded to meet. Even in the Christian religion, the Bible foretold that the prophets had foreseen the coming of Christ – that is, the birth of Jesus Christ. The entirety of Judaism rests on the Talmud, the book of prophecy, and Islam also recognises the prophet Muhammad.

When we go through the history of civilisation, we can encounter very old records carved in the walls that have elements of prophesying – the ancient Egyptian prophets who are respected as deities, Roman and Greek priests with whom the military leaders advised before large-scale warfare. It is also known that the Celts had their priests who lived in places outside the settlement, away from the ordinary world, where they dealt with, among other things, profanation. Their decisions and what they 'saw' would happen in the near future were respected by the elders.

There is almost no ancient civilisation, people, or religion that does not deal with prophesying or psychoanalysis. In many religions, we encounter various rituals that have elements of divination. Essen, the religious community of ancient Palestine, left behind files that provide a clear picture of their beliefs about their own ability to predict the future. There is indeed a great number of religious movements through history – but also those that exist today – on the basis of which the prophecy follows or the 'prophet' 'sees the future'. 'Watching the stars' or astrology is also one of the methods of 'explanation' of our past and future.

In South America inhabited a tribe that had the ritual of cutting off the head after physical death because they believed it would capture one's spirit that stepped into the future. The heads would be knocked onto stakes and placed in a circle around the settlement to get various information from them as to whether it would be raining, whether they would be attacked by another tribe, whether the hunters would have a good catch, and the like.

One of the most famous prophets in the history of mankind is Nostradamus. The whole study was written based on his prophecies. His predictions are printed in millions of copies and still enjoy great popularity. Considering the fact that this book was first printed in the middle of the sixteenth century, we come to the conclusion that people have believed, for several centuries, in what he claimed. However, if we look closely at this and similar books, we will never find the exact date of an event – day, month, year – the exact name of a person related to an important event, and the like.

In the field of social consciousness of the ancient man, intuition played one of the most important roles in the survival process. Regardless of whether it has been linked with visibility, it is quite certainly a useful tool for accessing unconscious sources of information that come from the immediate environment. But it is not necessary to mix intuition and clairvoyance. Intuition is a special state of consciousness that opens the possibility of accessing only a small amount of information, while clairvoyance refers to a specific set, often infiltrated or requested information about something.

There is not a small number of recorded cases in which it is certainly possible to get information that is completely unknown to all while the individual is completely ruling and coming to them. It is quite possible that the human brain, in a given state, can receive a range of information. As is well known, in hypnosis, one can recall the exact number of steps that pass from the door of their apartment to the office where they operate.

Often in a state of hypnosis, a person can 'extract' information, such as the exact number of books on the shelf or the colour of the clothes worn by a salesman in a shop where he bought food a few years ago, in doing so not knowing when and why he 'collected' such information. A similar process takes place when receiving information from people who are blind. It's about collecting information through certain channels using the code used in that process. Sometimes, completely unconsciously, a person can 'do it', and even that person does not know from where they have such 'abilities'.

RTS: Can we reliably distinguish false psychics from people who can really collect a certain amount of information about something or someone through deliberately focused attention?

GSF: Who has all the information, even that which is related to our future? My answer, from the very beginning, is the Creator. I'll tell you – *do not* allow intelligence and common sense to offend you 'prophets' and 'psychics'. Many in your place, just like you, now wonder how I can categorically claim it. Here's the simplest explanation. If it is possible that there are those who guess everything, 100 per cent, about what will happen in the near or distant future, we would have a large number of 'hits' on sports betting, for example.

I do not know a person who would bet a million dollars and say, 'If you guess the exact result of this and that game, a million is yours,' and that person who 'reliably knows the answer' does not say that at the same time – or, even simpler, sit in a casino and hit winning combinations in horse racing, soccer championships. Why not? Millions would be missing? Why don't they find mines of gold, oil, hidden treasures? Why don't they find the wanted criminals for whom millions of awards are issued? Or even simpler – bring me a 'psychic' and ask him to tell me the bank account number of my acquaintance or friend whom I accidentally choose at that moment – with a $1 million prize offered. The moment that happens, I will say something different from this.

It is characteristic of the human race that it possesses intuitive hints in the form of assumptions about what might happen. Rarely, this is 100 per cent matched, projected, and achieved. But we must not allow this fact to deceive us, and we attach to it the possibilities for a person to be able to know what is rightfully expected for us in the near or distant future. It is not inherent to any human being. If yes, you would have, at this moment, at least one person who can give you 100 per cent accurate answers to all questions, with exact figures, colours, shapes, and so on.

There is a worldwide Science and Sceptical Inquiry organisation that offers millions of dollars to prove its 'clairvoyance'. According to the results published so far, this test, lasting only thirty minutes, has not been passed. Why? Loverhood is just as expensive to pay everywhere, all over the planet. If we could somehow collect the funds that the 'psychics' got, it would be a huge sum of money that I cannot even imagine – I believe bigger than any world fund.

Indeed, there are too many examples of the abuse of such 'abilities' around the world. I have already mentioned one of the most famous people in the world who dealt with a lot of abuse. It's about Vanga. A whole team of Russian scientists studied her abilities. Vanga had had at least a million people visiting her during her fifty-five years of psychic service. According to her vision, hundreds of people were waiting in line in front of her house in an attempt for her to predict their future.

Information about one of the most famous prophets is twisted because of so many stories and legends. There is even a cult of Vanga and also an organised group that initiated the process for her canonisation by the church. The Sector of the Apologetic Mission of the Synodal Mission Centre of the Russian Orthodox Church has explored this phenomenon in detail. On the basis of everything, they filmed a documentary titled *The Truth about Baba Vanga*, which, in many ways, illuminates her 'psychic' abilities.

Namely, Vangeliya Pandeva Gusheva, the world-famous Vanga, received for decades people in the home in which she lived to 'see' their lives. It is known that even in 1967, in Bulgaria, as a citizen, she registered her activity and received a salary for the state. In a way, it was part of Bulgaria's tourist offer at that time, an attraction unique in the world.

There were official tariffs that were paid to the open account of all those who visited Vanga. Citizens of Bulgaria paid ten leva, citizens of former socialist states paid twenty leva, and citizens of Western countries paid $50. So the people who visited Vanga also made the state. Which means that the state gave her full legitimacy and the 'green light' to deal with the 'psychic'. In doing so, Vanga had many followers who allegedly recorded her prophecies. By insight into one part of the record, at first glance, it can be said that most of her statements are given with one dose of arbitrariness, i.e. uncertainty.

Whether the data that was given was accurate or incorrect and which individuals were concerned, this cannot be determined only by insight into the recorded document. It would be necessary to investigate in what percentage her allegations about the future of an individual were correct, and this requires time and the will of an individual to tell the truth about their personal experience with her.

However, there is written evidence found among individuals in the possession of the Russian state. In one of the records held as official documents in Russia, Vanga predicted that the USSR, a former federation of Russian states, would enter with its army in Chile in 1973, which, of course, did not happen. Among other things, she predicted that Bulgaria would join the Soviet Union in 1993, which did not happen. It was said earlier that the world would enter into conflict in 1960 – that is, she predicted the beginning of the Third World War, which, again, did not happen. For 2011, she predicted an ecological cataclysm because of the disintegration of radioactive particles in the northern hemisphere or the disappearance of the plant sand animal world, which, again, did not materialise. Numerous 'pumped' journalistic stories have greatly helped in the promotion. The marketing made Vanga a world star – 'a clown who infallibly predicts what the whole world is expecting, not just individuals'.

A similar story is observed with other 'mysterious prophets and psychics'. They enjoy great media support, and not rarely are their promoters famous personalities or the state itself, as was Vanga's case. A distorted picture of reality, feeding human curiosity, promoting a projected future, call it whatever you want to have a common denominator – its name is 'bananas'! This is, perhaps, a milder word for fraud, but basically both refer to the acquisition of money for the lover of the most ill or desperate.

You will agree that consumers of psychic services are not only unenlightened and uneducated people but also those highly educated but in desperation. They seek help from such people, hoping to receive the answer or help they are looking for. Making money on human weaknesses is a great game that has existed since the beginning of human civilisation. One of these 'games' is also clowning.

Emptiness and hope often make people believe what they are 'serviced' in a very skilful way. Collective empathy, which later turns into euphoria, plays a major role in the promotion of such persons. To clarify, I do not claim that she has never succeeded in getting information through a communication channel and a code for obtaining certain information, but in most cases, it is mischief of a superstitious nation.

Vanga's claim to communicate with demons and obtain information from them is very similar to the state of obtaining information during sleep or a state of hallucination. But provided, she was telling the truth. A small number of cases is true. Based on the record of one of Vanga's followers, who was her great devotee, the 'angelic angel', we can have some sort of insight into how Vanga claimed to 'collect' information. She claimed that her voice, 'as if on the phone', was talking about the facts that only she carried on to people around her. Vanga argued that during the night, those 'forces' were forced to do some senseless things like wiping out wives, stripping and re-dressing them, and so on. All this points to the kind of trance in which one falls and one form of hallucinatory behaviour.

Like Vanga, many so-called psychics deceive people in seeing the future without fail, find missing persons, and so on. 'Clairvoyants' attach very often to themselves the ability to 'collect' accurate information about people and events or give the correct answers to questions about an object. I wonder then if they are really able to 'see', as they claim. Why then have none of them seen where certain war refugees were found, for whom an international red warrant was issued and huge amounts of money we offered to find them? These 'great psychics' often announced the date of a cataclysm each year, wars, conflicts between states, assassinations. They even had great media support in these public deceptions. People are prone to forgetting, and over time, they pass over missed forecasts. Although these 'forecasts' have never come true, people still believe their deceptions.

On the other hand, I ask the question 'Why didn't one of these "psychics" foresee the exact date of the beginning of a war?' Or 'Why did no one predict the date of the demolition of the Twin Towers?' Desiring profits and sensationalism, they often made lies easier and targeted individuals from public or political life as the persons to whom they 'prophesied' the future. In this way, they create an image of themselves with divine powers and knowledge, which is unacceptable.

Of course, if you ask them why they did not do these things, if they can 'see' where the missing persons are, they would say that sometimes some inexplicable force has told them not to interfere in these things. Visibility is, in fact, the belief that certain individuals have the ability to observe things from a vantage point. Visual persons are considered to be those who, without physical presence, can 'see' objects or the future.

Most of the claims about visibility are fiction because no one can objectively confirm everything that they say will happen in the near or distant future. Various predictions of 'psychics' and 'prophets' are mostly post festum or after some event, though they claim they have predicted them. Regardless of the huge number of manipulators and those who mislead the world around them that they are 'given by God to see and foretell', one should not overlook the fact that the human brain is largely unknown to us, as well as the way of receiving and processing information.

We have discovered only a fraction of a big enigma called the human brain, based on which we can claim that the reception of information and their processing is a process that is indeed partly happening. The human brain receives and processes information, stores it, and, if necessary, processes it. Any kind of oscillation from the usual processes, classical science is still exploring, although it is largely experimenting with 'artificial intelligence' and the like. Scientists are playing with the life of man, like self-paced psychics with gullible people.

As you know, there are people who are simply dependent on someone else's opinion. They are very suitable 'light targets' for manipulation. Looking for the 'truth' that awaits them in the 'future', they go with various guitarists, psychics, super-sensors who 'discover' what will happen to them. Over time, people who use the services of various 'psychics' becomes dependent on someone telling them what to expect. This dependence is similar to other addiction diseases, such as, for example, gambling addiction. Not infrequently, people who often visit different 'psychics' fall into paranoia, and occasionally suffer from schizophrenia. I have had many such cases in my practice.

Many of these 'psychics' have mastered various techniques of deception so that those who visit them leave convinced that everything they tell them is true. The process of curing people who have been exposed for a long time to the influence of the widening of 'psychics' and the emergence of rational thinking and behaviour is very tiring. Reprogramming can take a long time.

Many world-class scientific organisations spent a great deal of money exploring the abilities of those who claimed to be psychic. It is a huge loss of material resources and time for research that has given poor results or has brought humanity into an even greater dead end. Even scientists have done numerous experiments with such people. However, everything is based on statistical analysis, with no concrete explanations and conclusions. None of the scientists has so far explained how and if this is possible.

RTS: And is it possible that there are people with intuitive abilities that are very close to what we call 'clairvoyance'?

GSF: I would not be right nor honest if I did not say that I firmly believe that this is possible. I have read hundreds of articles, studies, and papers that deal with it, but a banal example of describing the 'visions of the future' before they appear is the novels of Jules Verne, for example. In *Twenty Thousand Leagues under the Sea*, he gave a detailed description and 'draft' of the submarine when it was almost unthinkable that a man could explore the maritime spaces and thus, not to mention some of his other works, where there are similar examples.

These are not just 'fantasies' of a writer. It is a romantic journey into the future with a concrete description of the objects. So according to the literary genre, it is classified as 'science fiction' and what Nostradamus wrote as a 'prophecy'. There are really many examples that people simply write about what they receive as information. It often transcends the genre and turns into a novel, such as with Verne, so as not to cause negative criticism, misunderstanding, or condemnation from the environment.

Let's start first on how we get information from the outside environment. Wherever we come from, the fact is that the information represents the received and understood constant, seeing as it has its own course. It would look like an image if we imagine that the reception of information takes place along the imaginary straight path. Until now, throughout the history of human civilisation, there had been a large number of those who claimed to be 'visionary', but most of them were limited by a combination of codes, i.e. complete information.

Therefore, I repeat – none of them have all the *codes*, or at least, the practice so far does not recognise the person who was able to receive all the information desired. In all this, one should not forget the fact that man – that is, the human brain – is not the creator of information but only its interpreter, someone who receives, modifies, transforms it according to their own possibilities and needs, as I already said, and again, I am underlining it. It should always be kept in mind that information, as a form of energy, is without time, shape. It is a higher dimension than one can think of, recognise, and define.

RTS: What is essential for the so-called opening of communication channels, i.e. getting information and processing them?

GSF: The features of human nature include the instinct for survival, and there are other instincts whose satisfaction is manifested through various behaviours. In search of solutions to go and fight through life, one often asks, 'Who am I? What will I expect in the future? How do I solve the problem?' In search of answers to these and similar questions, he often unconsciously enters the sphere of information in which certain laws govern the reception of information.

Hence, we can often hear comments like 'I knew it would happen', 'I just saw that it would be', 'I always knew it was a solution', and the like. Therefore, a person often searching for answers to certain questions or solutions, completely unconsciously, opens the communication channel, and with the help of the received code, mostly only once, comes a response from sources that are nothing but an informational field that is timeless and with an infinite number of existing information.

Many of us were, at one time, in a situation where we were intensely thinking about a particular question or searching for a solution, as if someone had 'whispered' the answer. Our usual reaction to this is 'I knew it'. Of course, there is the possibility that a person is fully aware of information through certain channels and received codes. I've seen that many times and made sure that this is possible. This kind of information is available to a small number of people.

By the way, I would like to mention something else. As it is possible to establish the process of obtaining information through communication channels and codes from the information field, it is also possible to narrow the field to that of another person and 'parasitise' his information field. I know that it is completely inconceivable to the general public that this is possible and that this is happening in our practice, but in the same way, the telepathy process that we talked about is actually the same principle.

But I would ask you not to misunderstand me. Expressed intuitiveness is one thing, and 'clairvoyance' is another. It is not inherent to a human being to have the capability of a telepath and to determine or clearly provide an answer to the question about everything that will happen. Despite the fact that it is completely natural and inherent in human beings to seek out and find answers related to a near or distant future, one should not be led by the claims of fraudsters who say they know the correct answer.

In the history of human civilisation, there were 'hits on the target' but never more than one in consecutive negotiation. The myths and legends of the prophets who have moved into all the pores of a human being, from religion to modern marketing agencies, live on the wings of the human need to know answers to all questions, to fight for life or the instinct for survival.

The misuse of the human psyche is one of the oldest forms of abuse and is most often applied in various forms. One of them is 'clairvoyance', and with this deception, we meet at every step through the history of human civilisation to this day. So I will repeat once again, emphasising the truth – having all the information about us and the world around us is unique to *only the Creator*.

9

Bioenergy — MIT or Reality

RTS: Today the term *bioenergy* is often used in everyday communication. There are many people in the world who talk about bioenergy. What do you think about it?

GSF: I will begin with determining the notion of bioenergy. It is always good to start from the beginning. The word *bioenergy* is of Greek origin, a coining of two words – *bios*, meaning life, and *ergon*, which means work. People often use words, although they do not know their true meaning. The term *bioenergy* is also used when talking about phenomena or activities that have nothing to do with bioenergy. Bioenergy represents the energy we possess and can exchange with one another.

RTS: Yes, we could, for example, define the term *bioenergy*, but I wonder what you personally think about the possession of bioenergy.

GSF: There are numerous practical exercises that find their methodology in bioenergy theory – such as tai chi, reiki, yoga, breathing exercises, deep concentration exercises – and they have different names for almost the same thing, depending on the climate in which they are based, to be transmitted through people and the media all over the world. I think that certain exercises can 'catch' a small percentage of bioenergy. I could say that there is a fashion in the world of bioenergy, which is a variable character, and it therefore changes the level of popularity of a certain technique.

Reiki, for example, is said to be a technique used to reduce stress and promote relaxation but is also a treatment in general. Reiki is a technique for unconventional energy treatment. The term *reiki* means 'cosmic energy'. It is the vital energy that keeps us vital on the planet. Life is simply an ongoing exchange of energy. Each system constantly exchanges energy with its environment. The term *reiki* in Japanese refers to the universal life energy that flows around us and in us and is now used in various meanings.

Reiki signifies the ability to channel universal life energy, and reiki also refers to the form and method of transmitting and applying this ability. The ability to activate universal life energy is instigated by the teacher of reiki by a so-called initiation. Reiki is learned in seminars as well as through most techniques based on energy guidance.

Reiki, in the teacher's state, awakens and strengthens everything that already exists. Reiki opens the door to our talents. Thus, it can make someone a healer and take someone else to the path of meditation, i.e. it opens new horizons for those who work creatively. The process is initiated by the activation of the symbol and by laying down one's hand on it, with the belief that life energy flows through people. If someone has low life energy, reiki can help him through illness and stress, and if they have high energy, the person feels healthier and happier.

Reiki simply allows us to carry more energy through ourselves. More energy automatically means more health, more success, more satisfaction, more love, and more happiness. All this is achieved through practice through the river. Reiki should mean balance. It is said to work at all levels – physical, emotional, mental, and spiritual. Reiki gives energy and heals the body. Studies suggest that it speeds up healing, reduces blood pressure, reduces stress, and lessens or removes pain.

For the transmission of reiki, the recipient does not have to do anything. They only have to be open inside and sit quietly. Transmission, alignment, initiation – regardless of how this procedure is called in different reiki circles – occurs simply as the teacher performs a certain process. When the initiation is done once, there remains the stage when the reiki is channelled for life. In this way, it is encouraged to advertise this method. At the heart of man is that he wants, and he is on the planet to be happy.

Advanced reiki entails learning more powerful symbols. It also teaches the creation of a crystal network through which healing energy can be sent without interruption of someone or something, through time and space. It can also be said that today reiki is one of the most popular methods of treatment and personal development in the world. There are many teachers in almost all countries. Scientific research is also carried out on the operation of reiki on bacteria and plants.

I claim that everything has already been seen. Only the names of techniques change. It is commonly known that a happy man is usually a healthy man. Today's way of life is fast and therefore shaky. Modern society is mainly for consumers, and human eyes 'ever hunger'. This is one of the reasons for the illness and loss of energy and hence the growing need of a man to adjust his needs and possibilities.

In a large number of cases, there is a disorder of that inner energy, and a person gets sick, whether psychologically or physically, depending on a case-by-case basis. There are few people who manage to stay in balance. From this, we make a simple conclusion that we live in a time where it is much easier to impose new methods of 'treatment', which are the same thing, only with different names, and I can freely say rituals.

I was thinking in a similar way about homeopathy. For example, it is said that homeopathy is an effective and scientifically based medical treatment method that stimulates the natural abilities of the human organism on the path of healing. Homeopathy stems from the fact that all conditions of disordered health reflect a disturbed balance in a person and that the sick man is the one to be treated, not his illness. Treatment based on homeopathic ideas began about two hundred years ago. The idea of such a form of treatment appeared much earlier, even in the time of old Greece, by Hippocrates.

It was only in 1796 that German physician and chemist Samuel Hahnemann formulated and systematised a different approach to the treatment of the sick, homeopathy, which is still in the 'experimental' phase to date. It is perfecting and looking for a new more advanced approach. The system called homeopathy is from Greek words that mean 'similar to suffering'. As did Hippocrates two thousand years ago, Hahnemann realised that there are two ways of treating a health disorder – a similar and opposite agent in relation to mood.

Take, for example, the case of insomnia. Treatment with the opposite means – used in conventional, allopathic medicine – implies that it is treated with the administration of an allopathic drug leading to artificial sleep. This often involves the use of high doses of drugs that can sometimes cause side effects or addiction. Another example might be that several people are treated with a cough with the same medicine – e.g. Benil, Olynth, Adrianol drops – and the causes of leech are usually quite different. Homeopathic treatment is a treatment for agents whose properties are similar to a picture of the disability of an individual patient, not the disease. It is given in very small doses – the minimum dose principle. For example, coffee in high doses causes insomnia in healthy people, while in very, very small doses, which is surprising, it can allow the patient to have natural dreams.

The official position of world homeopathy is that homeopathic agents cannot cause side effects and cannot become addicting. Innumerable clinical trials have been performed to prove the contrary, but the testimony has been confirmed. Better to say a homeopathic agent either works or does not work, i.e. the homeopath does not accurately determine the condition of the disability.

I was inevitably asked several questions. Who is then a homeopath? Doesn't he do the same thing as bioenergetics, reiki masters? How safe is the complete truthfulness of the patient's story? Does it mean that if he misses the estimate, healing will not occur? We know that homeopathic agents contain an infinitely small amount of the active substance in a specially prepared form.

Homeopathic remedies are made from plants, minerals, animals, vitamins, allopathic drugs, hormones, various tissues, or other sources such as magnets, light, colours, or sounds. The instructions for preparation are described in the appropriate pharmacopoeias. Homeopaths gives the patient a homeopathic agent that is a picture, a matrix of its condition – the principle of similarity.

He observes the patient as a complete person – that is, all his individual characteristics, emotional, mental, psychological, and physical. Homeopaths take the case by interviewing a person who complains about some health problems, and this interview lasts about one and a half hours. Based on selected, sometimes unusual questions which are not relevant to conventional medicine, the homeopath evaluates the case and determines the therapy after analysis.

It may happen that the homeopathic remedy is not overwritten immediately after a few days, i.e. after a detailed analysis of the patient's case, such as in chronic cases, because homeopathy takes into account some personality traits such as temperament, lifestyle, the environment in which one lives and works, non-verbal symbols, archetypes, etc.

Homeopathy is useful in acute disorders, epidemics, and infections, in cases of physical trauma or injuries. It is also useful in treating various types of addiction. In fact, according to Hahnemann, its application is unlimited. Doesn't all this sound familiar to you as well as other alternative approaches to treating a patient?

RTS: Yes, it really does. Would you tell me something about Juna Davitashvili? I would say that she is the precursor of the expansion of various bioenergetics around the world. As far as I know, you had a couple of meetings with her.

GSF: I could cite more examples of other treatments, which I will probably do during further discussions. But I would like to next mention this. The Russians were, about forty years ago, the first to term bioethics. More specifically, during the seventies, the Russian intelligence service, the KGB, began to cooperate with a woman who was engaged in pursuing and raising herself to the level of a superman. It was about her superpowers.

It was the famous Eugene 'Juna' Juvanevna Davitashvili – born 22 July 1949, and died 8 June 2015 – a native of Georgia who came to Moscow in the 1980s, where she became the most famous Russian healer and bioenergetic healer for politicians and celebrities from Russia and from all over the world. She lived and worked in anonymity all the way to perestroika in Russia. She claimed to cure cancer and many other serious illnesses, even if she was able to prolong life for over a hundred years. She has relied on a lot of officials from the former Soviet Union, Soviet artists like Ilya Glazunov and Arkady Raikin, as well as world stars like Robert De Niro and Marcello Mastroianni.

Knowing that the Westerners were religious, they projected her as a woman with secretive forces and energy, so she became a world-renowned bioenergetic. According to one rumour, Juna was brought to Moscow from the Georgian secret service to rescue the sick and errant Brezhnev, and if the doctor dealing with the health of the aforementioned Brezhnev, the famous cardiologist and academician Yevgeny Chazov, claimed that Juna and Brezhnev had never met – bearing in mind that remedies are possible – such assertions should not be questioned.

When the USSR collapsed and when chaos took place in the country, Juna organised the International Academy of Alternative Sciences, which she headed. Later, she became the 'vice rector' of the Open University of Non-Traditional Medicine in Columbia, formed by emigrants from the USSR. She received a lot of awards, certificates, and patents for her work, and the Order of Folk Friendship was handed to her personally by then president of Russia Boris Yeltsin in 1994.

Things began to change a little bit as healing began, and they hired scientists to see what was actually going on. Her results were also noted in the case of unpaid patients. However, there has been one conclusion – which is, in principle, a placebo effect. The media did their own work, and only individual cases were presented. However, they were quite rare. People who were treated with classical medicine with Juna's bioenergy were presented. The cause of healing could not have been attributed to Juna!

RTS: Will you explain to me more closely what the placebo effect is?

GSF: The word *placebo* in Latin means 'to satisfy, to be happy'. The term *placebo domino* is also found in the Bible, which, in translation, means 'please the Lord'. Interestingly, the term *placebo* was also used in the fourteenth century, referring to mourners who would falsely complain and mourn the deceased during burials to get food and drink in return. Only in the second half of the eighteenth century did the word *placebo* appear in the *New Medical Dictionary*, describing marginal practices that aim to 'satisfy' the patient more than to cure him.

Today the notion of the placebo effect is already well-received in medicine and is a way to observe the effect on the patient when given a fake drug without any effect on the body and without them knowing. It is also used in the examination of the effects of new drugs. Then the test is done on several patients. One group of patients is given the right drugs, and the other group's, the control's, drugs are the same in shape but with completely harmless and useless content, which is not known to the respondents. After a certain time, the operation of genuine and false drugs is compared.

The placebo effect, unfortunately, has become frequently used by pseudo-science in the sense that it explains the functioning of all alternative therapies. Also, various charlatans actively spread misinformation about the placebo effect itself as something mystical and unexplainable. It is often associated with the power of 'positive thinking', which uses the mechanisms of self-healing of the organism. All this knowledge has led me to constantly think about how much a person is actually a remedy for himself – of course, with help – because we often do not see ourselves well, while someone appointed or 'predestined' does not open up to us about something else.

RTS: Yes, it is now understandable, how it came to cure people. Will you tell me something else about Juna and her followers, if we could call them that, who still appear today in a large number of countries?

GSF: Juna was a very good actress, and she knew how to leave an impression on the patient. The influence of the 'magic' that she was organising with an unknown ritual, which she designed on the spot, was astonishing. The first time I had met with Juna was in 1988 in Moscow, and the last time was in 1999, also in Moscow. Our last conversation was very open in the atmosphere of a pleasant restaurant.

Then to me, Juna confirmed what I had thought. I really was not in agreement with what Juna was representing because I was familiar with what she was doing and how much the percentage really was of the alleged healing of the people who came with her. She was undoubtedly charismatic, unusually dressed, and selling her imagination well.

Juna was an institution. In her schools, she allegedly trained other people to use their bioenergy for large sums of money. With the certification, new bioenergetics were further 'treated'. After a couple of days at the Juna course, they would later work and 'cure' independently, taking money from people who wanted healing. The notion of the famous bioenergetic engraved in my memory is as follows. 'Who am I to God's promises to change?' She knew it was impossible. She told me herself that the price of her treatment was 'treated'.

RTS: What are you saying?

GSF: Juna told me directly, 'The price is my medicine, and the amount of honours for my services is the single reason that meets improvement.' I've been thinking about it a lot, and I'll give you a couple of examples. In the shoe store, at the highest rack, shoes were placed that cost $1,000. In the lowest rack, there are identical shoes with a price below $100. There was a guarantee on the shoes of the upper shelf and not on the shoes from the lower shelves. Complaints on the shoes from the bottom shelf were numerous, and no complaint came to the shoes from the upper shelf.

Another example is that one group of participants in an experiment were told that they would receive a new drug that cost $2.50 per pill. Among the members of this group, the vast majority reported that the pill significantly reduced the pain of shocks. The other group was told that it was a new drug whose price was recently reduced from $2 per pill to ten cents per pill. Only about half of the participants in this second group reported that the pill helped them.

So in practice, it is often confirmed that the price of a drug directly affects our belief in its effectiveness, i.e. it leads to a direct link between price and efficiency – the higher the price, the higher the efficiency. In some studies, it has been shown that other additional elements can be further manipulated by the perception of pain. For example, if the participants in a study come to see a professional doctor in a white coat, the pill for them works better, but if a salesman dressed in jeans and a regular T-shirt comes to the door, the pill is far weaker.

In other words, our perception – from the Latin *perceptio*, meaning, from a psychological point of view, all those mental processes that are directly caused by sensory stimuli – cannot only produce the effect, the reduction of pain, in addition to the pacemaker's pill. Through seemingly unimportant things, we can influence the level of this therapy.

On top of that, additional studies have shown that the same effect also occurs in real medicines, those that have an impact on the physiology of the organism. Doctors with neat and professional practices have more patients than doctors who work in unhealthy and unprofessional settings, not only because of their looks and style but because the drugs work better on the transcript.

In needle treatment, several smaller acupuncture studies have shown that it significantly helps with certain types of pain in the joints and muscles. Hence, some wondered if there might be truths in the old Chinese story of chi that flows through certain lines and which can become the cause of the disease if the proper energy flow is interrupted.

To check this, several major studies were organised. Patients were randomly divided into two groups and sent to go to two different groups of acupuncturists. One group consisted of 'real' acupuncturists, masters of traditional Chinese medicine. They nailed the needles in the chi meridians according to the ancient rules of this method of treatment. The other group consisted of 'fake' acupuncturists, actors who nailed patients with needles.

RTS: And what happened?

GSF: Patients reported a significant reduction in symptoms. Acupuncture helped them a lot – but equally for both groups. Therefore, needle stitching is enough to help a person, and the knowledge of Chinese medicine and of chi meridian is not necessary at all to achieve certain results.

RTS: Is the needle pinch really so medicinal?

GSF: I made the conclusions based on the mass of examples which I myself saw but also read. I will cite another example of a study that tested whether acupuncture helps women who suffer from menopause. The scientists sent a group of patients to a false acupuncturist who not only deliberately chose the wrong place to hack but was also using fake needles. The specially manufactured needle would touch the skin, but it would never hurt them, and it remained in place only because of a small piece of sticky tape.

RTS: What was the result?

GSF: Many patients experienced significantly reduced symptoms, just like those who went to the 'real' acupuncturists. The mere fact that they went to therapy in which they trusted was enough to make that therapy effective. Parkinson's disease is a very serious neurological disorder in which a critical group of neurons in the deep brain slowly die. This extinction leads to a number of effects, from cognitive to emotional, although most physically visible – the patient has difficulty moving, the body occupies a typical posterior position, and the stroke turns into alternating pulling of the foot along the floor.

Although there are drugs that can relieve Parkinson's symptoms, their effectiveness slowly decreases over time, until eventually, they become virtually unusable. One way in which the disease can be reduced or eliminated, independently of drugs, is so-called deep brain stimulation, a technique in which electrodes that impose electrical impulses change the activity of damaged structures and facilitate voluntary movements.

What's astonishing is that the placebo effect works even in this case. The operation is performed, and the electrode is inserted into the patient. They get involved, and they work. The patient can move normally. Then within the system setting, the implant is temporarily switched off, and the patient immediately restarts. But now the doctor can perform a trick – he tells the patient that he turned on the electrodes again, even though he did not do it. The result is that the patient can suddenly move completely normally. Although he still lacks the necessary neurons, even though the electrodes are completely inactive, all of a sudden, it works just as it should, just because the patient believes the implant is turned on. Unfortunately, this effect is temporary. After a short period, the effect stops again, and the only way to restart normally is that the electrodes must really be activated.

RTS: The example is over, and we will talk about them in further topics. Tell me what official medicine says about everything we are talking about. Is it not normal to draw a conclusion that it is necessary to deal more with these effects, and do you think it really makes sense?

GSF: Official medicine has never recognised nor verified bioenergetics, i.e. as a treatment agent, but it has recognised acupuncture and hypnosis, although on the basis of the examples presented, that can be said that in all treatment methods. The placebo effect has a lot of share for one single reason – because it does not work, and it's not what it is. For individuals, eventually, the results were achieved thanks to the placebo effect.

There was never a single bioengineer employed in any hospital in the world. Their centres are completely 'private'. Western medicine knows the phenomenon of life energy. It does not deny this, but it does not officially recognise it. Even the alleged bioenergetics themselves do not know the cause of the rare cure. They gain the conviction that it is only thanks to them. However, this is not a basis for the claim.

In most cases, big money is at stake, which is earned when self-condemned 'healers' do not give up. A large number of patients going to bioenergetics were under the therapy of classical medicine. When they miss the desired results, even in parallel with the therapy prescribed by the doctor of classical medicine, they go to the bioenergetics.

It happens that after two or three sessions of bioenergetics, there is a cure or a significant improvement in the condition of the patient, but the patient himself cannot attribute his cure to the 'guru'. The media plays an important role in the whole story. Bioenergetics and a number of patients transmit their experiences to the media and talk about healing. Until now, there is no known system or method of using this energy. Excepting suggestive effects, the energy of life or bioenergy is present and functions according to its unknown laws, and it maintains complete life on the planet – man, flora, and fauna.

Temporality, inconsistency, and unpredictability greatly hamper the understanding and use of placebo. For modern medicine, it is mostly an accidental side effect, something that requires additional studies and checks. If a sugar tablet can treat a person a little, then how do we know the effect of the actual tablet? We should do endless studies that compare the effectiveness of the right drug with the effects of the placebo. If there are cases of healing in the application of various techniques of alternative medicine, how can we really be sure when we will really be cured, and what is the most effective?

RTS: Can you explain a little bit more about time, inconsistency, and unpredictability when applying bioenergy or any other method of treatment?

GSF: The first problem is temporality, which is nicely illustrated in one of the examples I mentioned. From the description, we might think that Parkinson's disease is, in fact, psychological and that we can treat it by making the patient convinced that he is not actually ill. But this conviction can only remove symptoms briefly. The brain can 'push for power' for some time, expecting electrode support, but after a while, this 'help through self-confidence' is no longer sufficient to outweigh the physical limitations of the patient's damaged nerve networks.

The second problem is inconsistency, which I will present with the example of hypnosis. In one clinical study, hypnosis proved to be very successful, treating up to 80 per cent of patients. The man hypnotises someone, suggesting that his nipples will disappear within two days, and two days later, the nipples disappear, as if they had never been there.

It is not so clear how this effect works, although new hypotheses suggest that hypnosis, in an unknown way, leads to a reduction in blood flow to the infected tissue, which is a 'starving' tumour. The data is still very preliminary, and this effect is still one of the larger mysteries. It works very well on nipples, which, in principle, are caused by the tumour. But in doing so, it does not work for other similar tumours. The elimination of adolescents through hypnosis has never left anyone around. Unfortunately, also, hypnotherapy in the fight against cancer has not proved to be effective.

The third problem is unpredictability. People who experience the placebo effect and know about it occasionally can have a strong placebo reaction, while at the same time, some of the people who sincerely believe that it is a real drug do not get any positive results. The reproducibility of placebo therapy is therefore very low, and it can never be predicted that any individual patient will react. In medical circles, it can often be said that alternative medicine actually does not exist.

Any therapy that proves to be effective is adopted in the framework of modern medicine. What turns out to be dysfunctional is rejected. Therefore, 'alternative medicine' is simply a way to say 'non-acting therapies'. However, the placebo effect makes this a little more complicated as through alternative approaches, it can produce seemingly real effects.

Homeopathy, for example, is based on ideas that are based on physics and chemistry and are completely unsustainable. However, it seems to be quite acceptable to the average person, and hence, homeopathic water and tablet tablets can act through the placebo effect. This, at first glance, does not look bad. Alternative medicine is a system through which a person can manipulate his subconscious mind and at least use his power of treatment somewhat. A few drops of water from the bottle of 'homeopathic medicine', a pair of needles by an acupuncturist, or a couple of treatments with bioenergy, and various problems based on immune psycho-neurological bases can be solved.

At the same time, in such problems, modern medicine is often impotent since therapies are focused on the physical causes that the patient does not actually have. This is realistic and can be said to be the 'bright side' of alternative medicine. But unfortunately, there is also a 'dark side', which paradoxically arises precisely from such occasional successful treatments.

Let's look at one typical situation, observing an alternative treatment from the perspective of an average patient who is not aware of the complications placebo produces. A man has suffered from occasional severe abdominal pain for several years. He went to various doctors and specialists but without success. Nobody could help him or find the cause of the disease. And then one day he goes to the acupuncturist, gets shaken, and becomes better. Then he goes again and again, and in the end, he is left with no pain, completely healthy.

What conclusions can we draw from this? Completely logical, a man can conclude the following:

- Doctors have no idea (for years have not managed to cure the problem)
- Acupuncture works
- Bioenergy really exists
- Classical medicine should be based on the control of chi
- Modern medicine makes mistakes in its approach

Add to this some minor purely statistical data that make modern medicine very scary to many people. Let's take chemotherapy for lung cancer at the last stage. Of twenty people who get this kind of cancer and then refuse chemo, we will see that within a year or two, all twenty will be dead. Death from this cancer is very slow and painful.

But what happens if we observe the twenty people who have received this kind of cancer and then accept chemotherapy? Nineteen of them will continue to die, striking both chemotherapy and its benefactors. Only one in twenty will survive. What are the effects of these statistics?

You see, we have nineteen families and a group of friends who have seen with their eyes how much the patient under chemo was very swollen and eventually died. There will be few who see death without chemo. They will suffer pain and suffering as a toxic drug. These nineteen families will talk about it to others and turn their heads in horror.

On the other hand, we will have only one happy family who sees that their father, mother, or cousin is swept under chemotherapy, but then they also win over the disease. As a result, horror stories about chemotherapy will be heard more often than curing stories. Here, we have a large number of people who believe that chemotherapy is the totally meaningless torture of people. Of course, this is not true. Ask that twentieth family if it is better that one in twenty survives or that everyone dies. But people are not aware of this, and hence, the basis for suspicion of medicine is created.

RTS: Tell me, what do you think further influences the frequent addressing to people who are dealing with alternative medicine, whether they are homeopaths, acupuncturists, reiki masters, or bioenergetics?

GSF: The often immoral behaviour of large pharmaceutical companies is putting oil on fire, giving further arguments that official medicine is really utterly incorrect. It is therefore not surprising that people are turning to cure the 'other side' in relation to classical medicine.

Modern doctors, who have many more patients, cannot invest the same amount of time in each patient as, for example, some bioenergetics, who, at the time, mainly charge large amounts of money. This does not mean that we should not try or that nothing can be learned from this contrast. A doctor may take an extra few minutes and explain the problem to the patient with an understandable language, explain how the prescription medication works and what effects the patient can expect. This little effort is sufficient to achieve a large part of the positive effects without the need to turn the review into a psychotherapeutic session.

Instead of taking authority as a kind of physical fact that radiates from a white coat, it would be good if a little more effort was invested in its production and maintenance. So at least, I think the effects of treatment and in classical medicine have greater success while reducing the departure of alternative 'doctors' who are 'multiplying' at an incredible rate and gaining material benefit without corroborating evidence that their therapy makes the patient better.

RTS: In addition to this, can something else be done?

GSF: Active prosecution and the banning of alternative routes in any general sense are not realistic and good options since such behaviour would only increase the already present paranoia against the medical system and push the alternative methods even deeper into the shadows, where malversations become even easier and bigger.

The better approach is the reverse – conditional support for benign alternatives, with education at every step. That would be one of the solutions. Public education on the nature of the placebo effect can also help. Understanding the placebo effect diminishes its effectiveness, but it does not eliminate it. Even the greatest unbelievers can occasionally see its fruits. An increased level of understanding can help people understand at least a little where modern medicine is in relation to the alternative.

For now, it did not go any further, even in an attempt. One day, when our understanding of the mechanisms of nature, even of human beings, becomes well enough, we will be able to manipulate them directly. For the time being, I have talked about the placebo effect as the only way to access certain mechanisms, and therefore, alternative medicine – bioenergy, acupuncture, reiki, acupressure – remains in circulation. I will reveal further to you the parts of my knowledge that I have come to discover.

RTS: Would you add more about dealing with alternative methods of treatment?

GSF: In all alternative healing treatments, I have to mention that there are a large number of charlatans and manipulators who are exclusively dealing with alternative treatment for profit. For the majority, I can claim that they do not possess even a fraction of the knowledge in the field they represent and which they are making. The marketing presents them as great masters and healers. In the media, they are providing information that they are miraculous creatures. Most of them claim that they had clinical deaths, after which they received a 'gift from the sky'.

There is another group of exploiters. This second group is paranoid religious or magical people who imagine their sick fantasies. They are unconscious of their actions and deceptions and also are convinced that they have the power, and it has nothing to do with reality. The result of their deceit is that their patients, pay a high price by neglecting therapies that could improve their health or cure them.

The mortality of patients going through such treatments is high. They justify it with the words 'It must have been so'. They charge large sums of money for their services and do not feel any responsibility when patients get worse or die. Throughout the world, there are holy places where people leave and where prayers and confessions are recommended as a method of treatment.

In these 'sacred places', on a daily basis, there are a large number of people who also leave large sums of money at so-called sanctuaries. I have visited some of these shrines, and I became convinced of my claims, as I had already described in the example of the Lady of Medjugorje.

10

Clinical Death

RTS: What is clinical death, and can a person receive and send information in such a state?

GSF: *Clinical death* is a medical term for the cessation of circulation and breathing, two essentials for maintaining human life and other organisms, the appearance of clinical tingling when the heart stops beating. Before the discovery of cardiopulmonary resuscitation or CPR, defibrillation, epinephrine injections, and other treatments in the twentieth century, the absence of blood flow as well as vital functions of the organism related to blood circulation is considered to be the official definition of death.

A cardiac arrest of a prolonged interval is called clinical death. In the medical practice, it is considered the final physical condition before the officially pronounced death. At the beginning of clinical death, consciousness disappears within a few seconds. Measurable brain activity disappears within twenty to forty seconds. The body is in a state of clinical death – that is, all tissues and organs are gradually subject to certain injuries that are called ischemic injuries.

RTS: What is death?

GSF: Initially, I want to briefly recall how science and medicine officially treat the phenomenon of death. Death – Latin *mors* – means a cessation of life. That is, an irreversible interruption of the life activity of an organism – plant, animal, human – i.e. the cessation of the existence of an individual as a separate living system. In medical terms, death practically represents the state of the organism after the termination of the work of the vital organs, the heart and the brain. Death is not an actual event but a process that takes time, and there are several different definitions.

Clinical death, as I have said, represents an irreversible and ultimate breakdown of cardiac and blood circulation and breathing processes. Short-term interruptions of cardiac work – e.g. in surgery, in general anaesthesia – do not necessarily lead to death as reanimation can be restored. When the heart and blood circulation stop, the cells in organs and tissues are active, metabolised, for a certain time, which is proportionate to their sensitivity and lack of oxygen. The most common in this series are ganglion cells in the brain cortex and then those in the basal ganglia of the brain.

If the cessation of cardiac output persists for more than four to five minutes, these cells die out, and cerebral death occurs. From cerebral death, it is necessary to distinguish decortication, i.e. the death of the ganglion cells. In such cases, the person is unconscious, but spontaneous heart activity and breathing remain. A few hours after cerebral death, cell activity in other organs and tissues gradually ceases. The latter are dying of epithelial airways and sperm cells, thirty hours after clinical death, and then biological death occurs. Shortly thereafter, biological death occurs, and the first changes are observed on the dead body, called the signs of death. There is also so-called apparent death, obscurity, which represents a state in which the basic life functions are reduced to a minimum and can take up to forty-eight hours.

Death is the subject of many philosophical, mythological, religious, aesthetic, artistic, and ethical debates. Plato still claimed in *Phaedo* that death is merely a 'separation of the soul from the body' but also a radical condition of absolute knowledge. Only completely separated from the body can the soul be again elevated to the level of pure supernovae of the idea. This view culminated in Plato's view that death is the best because it is precisely through which the soul can be completely cleansed.

Contrary to such claims, Epicurus argued that the death of a physical person at the same time also meant the cessation of all human psychic functions. He pointed out that according to death, we can be completely indifferent. 'For as long as we exist, there is no death, and when death comes, then we no longer have ourselves.' The rhinoceros religion of death shows predominantly the punishment or the consequence of the transgression of sin, e.g. Tertullian, Augustine.

Later Christian writers – e.g. Thomas Aquinas, Duns Scotus – emphasise the thesis that death is the return of the body to the matter from which it was created and souls to eternal life. Leibniz considers that death is nothing more than a gradual involvement of the body, and Fichte claims that death is, in fact, only a correlative notion of life, i.e. the 'negative side of life'. According to Hegel, death is the highest 'universality' that an individual is reaching. Arthur Schopenhauer treats death and birth only as 'vibrations' of eternal living ideas, so 'when a man dies, a world, but only one that he carries in his head, collapses'.

From the many ideological views, Hebbel's claim is characteristic – 'death is the sacrifice that a person is wearing the idea of'. Biologist H. Driesch argues that 'death can only be an entry into metaphysics of more than one kind'. Mr Simmel points out that 'instead of a time-consuming conflict of life and death, it should be pointed out that there is a single endless existence in which death and life intertwine as the rings of a single chain'. F. Nietzsche argued that the act of dying is not as important as that physiology and theology attributed to man, which also implies the assertion that in 'reality, there is not a single banal matter of death'.

The philosophy of existence in various interpretations – from S. A. Kierkegaard to M. Heidegger, G. Marcel, and A. Camus – regards the phenomenon of death as one of the fundamental problems of philosophy, even 'the only real problem of philosophy', and the concern for and fear of 'disease to death' become important preoccupations in contemporary Western European philosophies. Heidegger's special features are viewed as a human being 'coming to terms with death'. Nikola Tesla claimed, as I have repeatedly stated during the conversation, that death does not exist. Robert Lanza, an American scientist and professor at the Institute of Regenerative Medicine at the University of Wake Forest in North Carolina, says, 'Many of us are afraid of death. We believe in death because we were told we were going to die. We connect ourselves with our body, and we know that the bodies are dying.'

However, a new scientific theory claims that death is not as much a final event as we think. One of the more prominent aspects of quantum physics is that certain observations cannot be predicted absolutely. Instead, there are a number of possible observations, each of which has a different degree of probability. One of the 'mainstream' explanations, the theory of 'many worlds', states that each of these possible observations corresponds to a different *univerzum* ('multiverse'). A new official theory called biocentrism deepens these ideas.

There is an unlimited number of universes, and everything that could happen at all happens in one of them. Death does not exist in the real sense in these scenarios. All possible universes exist simultaneously, no matter what happens in any of them. Although individual bodies are destined to self-destruct, the feeling of life – the question 'Who am I?' – is only a fountain of energy of twenty watts that occurs in the brain. But this energy does not disappear with death. One of the most certain axioms of science is that energy never dies and cannot be destroyed. But does this energy transcend from one world to another?

Let's take a look at an experiment recently published in a journal that says that scientists can retroactively change something that happened in the past. The particles have to decide how to behave when they come across the air separator. Later, the experiment conductor could turn the other switch on and off. It turns out that what the observer decides at that moment determines what has happened in the past. Regardless of the choice that you, as an observer, make, you are the one who will experience the consequences that follow. The links among these various histories and universes transcend our usual classical ideas of time and space. Imagine a twenty-watt energy that simply holographically projects one or the other on the screen. Regardless of whether the second air separator is switched on or off, it is still the same battery or agent responsible for the projection.

According to biocentrism, time and space are not solid objects as we think. Wipe your hand through the air. If you take everything, what will stay? Nothing. The same thing is related to time. You cannot see everything through the bones that wrap your brain. Everything you see and experience at this moment is the source of information that happens in your mind. Time and space are only tools for assembling a whole. Death does not exist in the timeless and infinite world. Even Einstein admitted, 'Now Beso has separated from his strange world a little in front of me.' It does not mean anything. People like us know that the distinction among the past, the present, and the future is only a persistent stubborn illusion.

Immortality is not a permanent existence in time without end, but it resides on the other side of time. Although this sounds very abstract at first glance, it should always be guided by the fact that time itself is a phenomenon for which there are a large number of instruments and mechanisms for measuring but that it cannot be said with certainty that any is correct.

RTS: How do most people experience death?

GSF: Most people think that after death comes paradise or hell. Some of them think that there is nothing after death. Old people believe that death is going to the eternal hunting ground, and that's why they bury their dead with tools, jewellery, and weapons needed for that eternal life. In fact, none of us really knows what comes after life or death. The scientific and academic discipline that studies the deaths of human beings is called thanatology, but it has not yet provided an adequate answer to numerous questions about this phenomenon.

To better illustrate the reception of death by man, we will mention some examples from the media. On 9 January 2014, the *Chronicle* wrote, 'We cannot know when and how it hits us.' We cannot be 100 per cent sure what exactly will happen at that moment, but there are some death settings that you may want to find out, and the *Huffington Post* has collected them all in one place.

There is a scientific explanation as to why a dying person's 'life passes before their eyes'. Instead of the brain 'deadening' before death, it is believed that this activity is actually growing, causing a state of heightened consciousness. It can initiate a number of things, either "the passing of life in front of the eyes' or 'the light at the end of the tunnel', all of which are aided by reducing the inflow of blood and oxygen into the eyes. Your body is embarrassed after you die. You probably heard that after death, hair and nails continue to grow, but that is not true. In fact, the skin accumulates and reveals a larger surface of the hair and nails.

Additionally, when you die, your body will likely have one or both of these effects, so depending on the sex, you may also ejaculate. This, of course, happens because of the cessation of the brain, which no longer 'keeps everything under control'. If you are a man and die facing down, blood is gathering in parts of the body closest to the earth, so there's a possible erection. And if you're interested in how long it takes to become a skeleton, after about a week, the skin can be easily removed, and after about a month, teeth begin to fall out, followed by everything else.

There is a possibility that we misunderstand when someone is actually dead. You probably heard about cases in which people were declared 'dead' and then 'return to life'. And this is exactly what new research is dedicated to, which deals with the possibility that we have a completely wrong impression when someone is actually 'dead'. In a few cases, people who have 'returned to life' could change the conversation that led them to moments when their brain did not show signs of life. This made scientists think that there is no 'instant death' but that it is a process that goes slowly while the individual functions are discharged.

RTS: How do you interpret the fear of death in spite of numerous claims and teachings that death does not exist or that there is life after death?

GSF: One of the biggest fears among people is to be buried alive. So much is the human fear of being buried alive in the grave that it even has its own name – taphophobia. The first recorded case dates back to the fourteenth century, while the last one was prevented by a lucky situation in 2005. Here, we are not going to deal with cases of deliberate premature burial in the form of some kind of punishment that can only fall into the wisest brain function, and we will not engage in voluntary burial when a person who lives is buried alive by his own permission. We will only deal with the possibility that a person 'dies' – that is, everyone thinks that he is dead, although he is still alive, buried under the ground, suddenly waking from clinical death in a coffin, where no one can to hear him.

Yes, this sounds so terrible and terribly not surprising that many psychological studies show that it is one of the most widespread and most intense human fears. This fear is so widespread that there are graves that have appeared more often since the eighties of the last century which the 'deceased' could open from inside in case they are alive. Even earlier, during the nineteenth century, there were numerous inventions, such as the bell ringing on the surface, which were connected with the 'dead' by a rope so that they could ring it and arouse people on the ground to inform them that they was still alive.

On a purely scientific side, people buried alive die of choking, dehydration, hunger, or hypothermia in areas where the climate is harsh. This, unfortunately, can take several days, long enough for a person to be fully aware of everything that is happening, the situation which he is in, desperate for the ability to be rescued from physical pain. Those who have survived this testify incomprehensible physical and mental suffering, expressed above all through claustrophobia, which they would never get rid of despite the best psychotherapeutic treatments.

The oldest recorded case of a man who was buried alive was from the fourteenth century and referred to the death of well-known medieval philosopher and Catholic theologian John Duns Scotus. Namely, when his tomb was opened, he was outside his coffin, and his hands were wrinkled and bloody as he tried to escape in vain to drag the door to himself. The escalation of these stories begins in the nineteenth century. I will mention only two examples on this occasion.

On 21 February 1885, the *New York Times* published a news story about a man named Jenkins from the Bankomb district who was found after an exhumation turned on his stomach with a bunch of rubbed hair and traces of scratches through the opening of his coffin. His family was 'disturbed by all sorts of criminal neglect' of the authorities. On 18 January, the *London Times* published a similar news about a girl named after Kolins from Woodstock in the Canadian province of Ontario who was found in a casket buried in a foetal position, with the cover of the coffin in which she was buried scattered in small pieces. The latest case was fortunately prevented. Namely, in 2005, the body sack was delivered to a funeral enterprise in the U.S. state of Massachusetts, only in the bag was not a corpse but a living man, unconscious, as the director of the funeral company had accidentally discovered. He immediately called for an ambulance and saved the unfortunate man.

As for the answer to the question you asked, nobody in the world knows it. The dead do not speak or 'speak aloud' about themselves. It's almost an identical story when talking about clinical death. The World Health Organisation acknowledges the phenomenon of clinical death and the possibility of revitalisation, and accordingly, a law was introduced to prevent the burial of the dead a minimum of forty-eight hours from the moment of death.

However, what is characteristic of clinical death is the experience of people who have survived and 'returned to life'. Almost all those who have experienced occult death claim that they had similar experiences – the feeling of bliss, the abandonment of their physical body, and the famous 'light at the end of the tunnel'. According to American scientists, this most probably arises from a rise in the electricity of our brain at moments when the body is in a life-threatening state.

Earlier, it was thought that during clinical death, the brain completely ceased to work, that its activity was minimal, significantly weaker than in a conscious state. However, the results of animal studies show that the opposite is true. 'Brain activity at the time of death is far stronger than in a waking state,' says Jimmo Borgzigin, a professor at Michigan University. A group of researchers at the Michigan University conducted their measurements with an electroencephalogram, an EEG, on nine anaesthetised rodents that experienced heart failure. For thirty seconds from the moment their hearts stopped beating, they recorded a sudden increase and strong coherence in high-frequency waves, so-called gamma oscillations. These brain waves are considered to be the basis of consciousness in people, in charge of helping to connect information from different parts of the brain.

On average, about 20 per cent of people who have survived heart failure claim that they experienced being 'close to death'. Skorosvy describes them as having experienced a 'reality more real than reality'. However, scientists have so far not been able to explain how these experiences arise and whether they are possible at all after the heart stops beating. The same results were obtained by the experts when they induced asphyxiation in animals or lack of oxygen in the brain.

Clinical death does not choose age, time, place, skin colour, religious belief, or nation. It is at any moment, at all points of the earth. As humans experience clinical death, it has been established that it is happening both to animals and to plants. The media have only recorded a small percentage of the phenomenon that occurs every day throughout the world. The term *clinical death* refers to a state that is not a definitive or biological death and can have two outcomes – reanimation or biological death. Much greater is the percentage of switching from clinical death to biological death.

An extremely small percentage is the return from clinical death to life, the restoration of organs and heart and brain impulses. In Stony Brook, New York, a man and his seventeen colleagues from the United States and the United Kingdom decided to deal with this topic. For four years, they had analysed more than two thousand heart failure cases or moments when the patient was officially dead. Of those patients, they managed to revive 16 per cent and talked with 101 people.

Clinical death is known throughout history and in all religions, and everyone explains it in different and unique ways. Many people who were on the verge of death claim to have had a substantial experience, seen strong light, or experienced indescribable bliss. 'Some people feel that this extraordinary experience has made it possible to deceive the other world,' says the book *Recollections of Death*.

The Bible does not say anything about such unusual experiences. But it contains some basic truths that clearly show that people who have experienced clinical death did not briefly step into the grave. Therefore, based on the experiences of those who have experienced clinical death, there is no evidence that these people were shortly in paradise or hell or that there was life after death. That's life. We all have the same potential, so in 'clinical death', no one receives special gifts, but they are the manipulations of people for their own interests.

RTS: Is it possible to measure the potential energy released at the 'moment of death' in a person?

GSF: From the philosophical point of view, biological death means the separation of the physical body and the energy of life, what they call souls. The latest research in quantum physics in the human body – where the functions of all organs, the heart, and the brain have ceased – was recorded with electric impulses of minimum strength.

Because of the inconsistency of the energy instruments and techniques that we managed to record, we will call them electrical impulses. Not knowing their characteristics and complexity, we noticed only minimal electric activities, while other activities for now are not known to us. Science has made stimulators only for this activity – pacemakers, defibrillators, which, in certain percentages, restore or maintain biological life.

By studying the 'energy of life' – called in religion *prana* or chi and in medicine the energy of life – I came to the realisation that energy, not yet understandable, is with an infinite number of characteristics. Until today, we have known and been accessible to only one feature that is known in science as the electrical impulse. It functions in all living beings – fish, amphibians, reptiles, birds, mammals – meaning the simplest to the most complex organisms.

My discovery reveals several more energy features. We can classify these characteristics into one group, but so far, we have characterised them as memory, motion, or teleportation. This led me to conclude that the absence of the 'energy of life' is biological death. In the cases of 'bringing' or enriching the body with energy that was absent and keeping it comes the revival of the body and organs and the activation of the physical functions of the organism.

In the phenomenon of clinical death, where there has been a resurgence, it is in fact the process of returning energy to the body – that is, the organs, tissues, and cells that so far have been 'only' spontaneous or accidental. The life energy that depends on the life of the biological body, the function of the organs, is not physically shaped and is absolutely independent of the body and organs, and as such, it is able to leave the body and organs and can return if it so wishes.

In the event of a return, there is the revival from clinical death. By reviving a person with the energy of life, she does not lose any of her abilities and her identity. So the revived person speaks the same language, does not experience amnesia, and does not lose their sexual identity, and no psychological changes are noticed other than the experiences during clinical death. The experience retained in the memory of a person is very impressive, inspiring the basic characteristic of cognition and the belief of immortality. This has been reported in all individuals who have had clinical death experiences.

So we arrive at an unmistakable conclusion that with the absence of the energy of life, the body, as the place in which it has functioned, loses its vitality and, as such, disappears. We know that energy has no physical properties – that is, it does not decrease and does not disappear. It's just changing places. We can also conclude that it is not transformed. It is immutable, indestructible, which is proven in the cases of its return to the human body. Nothing is lost from the memory, which shows that neither character nor identity has changed.

The physical or biological body of a person does not 'decide' about the characteristics and activities of energy, its length of presence, and any changes of the energy itself. The effect is exclusively energy on the human body, while, conversely, it is absolutely impossible. Only the energy of life decides on the length of a man's life. Energy possesses intelligence, and the characteristics we have observed are that it is the carrier of memory, that it has the ability to change places and go beyond time capabilities – it is not limited by space or time – to decide on the place of functioning and the length of its functioning at a particular place, and it has the possibility of teleportation, which will be discussed later.

I have been thinking for a long time whether it is 'smart' to list, in my opinion', the most famous example in the history of mankind – that of Jesus Christ and his resurrection. Daily examples of clinical death and resuscitation confirm unequivocally and show us that the revival of the 'dead' is possible and that this is not a fantasy from the scriptures. Also, observing the phenomenon of revival in the context of modern times, I think that it is not accidental and that it has a strong message about the existence of the energy of life and its power. It is no coincidence that even that happens to a person, and there is still decipherment to be made of why it is 'there' and why exactly that person is chosen.

It is known that those who survived clinical death – that is, 'rising from the dead,' which is single-handed jargon – after this experience are dedicated to intense spiritual work and to the 'mission' of witnessing that death is not the end. The statements of experience are mostly based on the claims that they felt blissful, describing the presence of warm energy and the divine atmosphere as well as the ultimate realisation that after biological death, they are transferred to a spiritual energy level. We will only list two examples of the experiences of people who have experienced clinical death.

Five years ago, a man had surgery, during which he died and was clinically dead for several minutes. His claims about the process that took place 'in front of his eyes' were as follows – 'I woke up somewhere. It looked like I was in the universe, but there was no star or light. I did not move. I was just there. I was neither hot nor cold. I was neither tired nor hungry. I remember thinking about my life, as though I had learned it from a book and some exclamation pointed it out. Whatever it was, it changed my mind about some things. I'm still afraid to die, but I do not worry what will happen after that.'

Another example is that while many remember an undefined empty space, a person who experienced clinical death after an allergic reaction had a different experience. 'I remember being sucked very slowly, as if I was going through water, and the darkness faded and vanished. At one point, I saw a garden. It was not full of flowers, just dust and a little grass. In the middle were two children, a boy and a girl. I had the feeling that I could choose whether to stay or go, but every time I tried to leave, I would stay in the same place. I was thinking about the reasons why I want to go back and realised that I did not want to leave my mother. After that, I managed to leave this place, and my clinical death lasted six minutes.'

This knowledge that we will elaborate on in further responses can lead to revolutionary changes in medicine as well as in philosophy, religion, and so on.

11

Memory

RTS: Bearing in mind all the previous interpretations of memory, to what extent do they coincide with your opinion and the one you met in practice?

GSF: Memory or memorisation is a process of conscious beings in which the nervous system permanently or temporarily stores certain data. Memory may be such that it can be reproduced later or reproduced in such a way that data cannot be reproduced but only recognised in re-encounters. In a wider sense, memory, as we know, can also refer to the storage of data in biological and technical systems – for example, computer memory.

The memory process can be conscious and unconscious. What makes memory possible is the plasticity of the nervous system. Even some organisms far more primitive than humans can remember. The ability to remember in living beings has evolved from the nervous system. There is more division of memory. According to one of them, memory can be sensory. In the short run, it can last a few minutes, and in the long run, it can last for years or a whole lifetime. Memory can be divided into declarative and procedural memory. An example of declarative memory is the knowledge of facts. For man, according to the current scientific knowledge, the large brain section (neocortex) is responsible.

In practice, we also encounter the so-called procedural memory, which includes skills that are performed automatically without special intellectual effort, such as swimming, cycling, dancing, and the like. These activities govern the subcortical structures of the human brain. Memory phases can be divided into three phases – learning, coding, and consolidating knowledge. These are some generally accepted claims about memory – that is, memory in the shortest terms and which each of us should know.

RTS: In what way is 'writing' information – that is, storing data in the brain in a physiological sense?

GSF: Unlike activities like speech, motor skills, or hearing, there is no special centre for memory in the brain. Memory is the result of the joint action of multiple brain regions. The question here is what would be the basic mechanism of memory at the level of neurons. Memories are stored in nerve cell compounds, the so-called synapses.

There are one hundred to five hundred billion synapses among one hundred billion human brain cells. Many of them are not static. They appear and disappear and change the efficiency of communication among adjacent neurons. This feature is called synaptic plasticity. Donald Hebb was the first scientist to claim that synapses alter the binding strength of neurons. This theory was experimentally confirmed by Eric Kandel, for which he received the Nobel Prize in 2000.

There are several forms of synaptic plasticity. They vary in direction (strengthening or weakening along the direction), duration (short-term or long-term plasticity), type synapses (homo or hetero synapses), and mechanisms of action. The activation of synaptic bonds leads to biochemical changes, which, in the long run, can cause structural changes in the association of neurons.

Some regions of the brain can be associated with certain types of memory. This is demonstrated by cases of loss of memory in the event of an injury. For example, short-term memory is realised in the prefrontal cortex. Long-term memory is shared by the cortex and sub-cortex regions of the brain. The brain, as one processor, works on these principles and functions so long as certain physiological or 'anatomical' disorders do not occur.

RTS: Tell us something about declarative and procedural memory from the angle of a hypnotherapist.

GSF: Declarative memory is realised in the whole neocortex, with episodes being remembered mostly in the right frontal and temporal zone, while the meanings are remembered in the temporal zone. No matter where information is stored in the brain, a key part of the brain is the hippocampus for memory reproduction. Medical cases have been reported in which patients with severe cases of epilepsy have had their hippocampi removed for the purpose of treatment. Although the procedure would achieve its purpose, these patients would experience anterior amnesia – that is, they would remember the past, but they could not remember anything new. With hypnotherapy, we can get the maximum in terms of memory recovery, but such a brain no longer receives and does not process new information.

Automated and prefrontal brain regions are involved in mastering routine procedures, but the most important centres are in the small brain sections and basal ganglia. For emotional memories and for the measurement of furious reactions, the most important role is played by the amygdala. Some forms of primitive learning, such as conditioning, e.g. Pavlov's reflex, can be applied to animals, even to those less evolutionarily advanced. The littlest brain section is the most important for this kind of memory. Modern science recognises diseases or memory-related disorders, such as amnesia, retrograde amnesia, anterogenic amnesia, acute amnesia, Alzheimer's disease, in a more mild or severe form, memory blockade, dementia, and the like.

RTS: In your practice, did you encounter memory that 'spills' with the provocation of certain emotions, the so-called emotional memory?

GSF: The process in the human brain in which the experience of the past causes emotions is called emotional memory, but also, by provoking certain emotions in man, we provoke recollection of certain events, i.e. we are provoking the information he has recorded somewhere and which is activated only when he experiences a kind of emotional shock or even mild provocation.

In practice, this is case by case, and there is no unified response model as there is no same reaction to different stimuli in different individuals. To study these phenomena, they mainly used animals. The most common are experiments where rats are conditioned by the fear of unpleasant stimulation – for example, by electric currents. These studies have shown that emotional conditioning in the brain is realised through two mechanisms – subcortically, that is, subconsciously, from thalamus to amygdala, and cortical, that is, consciously, from thalamus through cortex to amygdala. The unconscious type is faster – 'something is hurting', 'I'm afraid'. The conscious type has a stronger long-term effect – 'it's a snake', 'it can bite me', 'I better get better'.

Neurotransmitter glutamate enables emotional conditioning by its action on the thalamus. Pathological nervousness is an abnormal activity in the amygdala and the hippocampus. It comes when harmless environmental stimuli are misinterpreted as danger. One of the typical examples of this disorder is post-traumatic stress. Because of a terrible event in the past, real or fictitious, a person experiences nightmares, apathy, and panic or fear of certain situations. It is likely that this person will turn to the abuse of alcohol or drugs.

Sometimes it was thought that memory, like muscles, could be practiced. It was considered that memory is one of the powers of the human spirit that can develop if it is used more. However, it has been experimentally proven that there is no improvement in memory capacity or the direct exercise of memory. Memory can be enhanced by improving the memory technique itself or by improving the state of the whole organism. It basically lies in providing sufficient oxygen for the brain, such as exercise or walks, and then taking several smaller meals a day to prevent blood vessel blockage etc.

For example, the world record in the memory of the largest number of pointless digits within five minutes is 396. I will mention something else that needs to be learned about the memory of the human brain. The memory is associated with each level of information processing. We distinguish three types of memory or memory functions:

1.   Sensory buffers memory
2.   Short-term memory or working memory
3.   Long-term memory

There are many scientific discussions and even disagreements about the details and/or boundaries of the division. But it is undeniable that these types of memory exist in our environment.

RTS: You've also been researching the memory of water. What knowledge did you come to?

GSF: It has been established by a series of scientific research in the council that has been carried out in laboratories in Russia, America, Japan, etc. By studying this, they came to the realisation that water has memory – that is, water has the capacity to remember. A well-known scientist, Dr Emoto Masaru of Japan, made specific experiments to prove it. Namely, he found that water was 'smart' by taking water from the same source and pouring it into several glass vessels. On one vessel, he wrote 'Love', on the second 'Thank you', on the third 'I'll kill you'.

In the fourth vessel was the water above which a prayer was read, and the fifth vessel was water without an indicated message. In addition to the written messages, he had said, 'I love you', 'thank you', and prayers for the health, happiness, and progress of oneself and their family, those who are guided by love, and as a killer, with great aggressiveness.

After a short treatment time, Dr Masaru analysed the water under the microscope. The results he came up with surprised only those who did not have the opportunity to come into contact with the works of Viktor Schauberger, a famous Austrian scientist, who, in the 1920s, claimed that water acts as a living being, that it has its own life and death, and that if we act improperly with it, it can 'get sick' and transfer its 'diseased' condition to all other organisms, plants, animals, and people. Emoto discovered that the water to which the words of love were referred made the most beautiful, bright, hexagonal star forms of crystals, while those who were referred to with hate words gave very irregular shapes of dark colour. So the chemical composition of the water did not change, but the clusters of water were differently grouped according to which words were sent to the water.

Another interesting experiment was worked out by putting rice and water in three glass containers. He addressed one vessel with love, attention, and harmony, the other with hatred, aggression, and unpleasantness, while leaving the third bowl completely neutral. After a very short period, he came up with fantastic results. In the first pot, to which he had spoken with love, the rice grew exceptionally well, with a healthy appearance and structure. In the second, to which he spoke with aggressiveness, the rice was completely black and ruined, and in the third, the neutral one, the rice began to grow slowly.

After these experiments, new creative ideas emerged, and the scientist began to examine the influence of music on water. He released Mozart, Bach, Beethoven, heavy metal, rock, and spiritual music and received for each type the different crystal formations indicated. This means that water 'hears' and 'remembers'. Russian scientists also experimented and still do it, so an interesting case happened in Siberia, in a military institute for the research and development of substances for mass destruction. The structure of water was studied on the basis of the molecules are connected and what molecular structure they make. It was noted that in every cell of water, there are 440,000 information fibres, which is really an incredibly large number.

There are a number of examples from everyday life where a person really influences water with his thoughts, desires, and prayers. It is known that the water prayed to by the monks and priests has the structure of hexagonal star crystals, while water taken from the same source that the monks did not pray to were completely different. If there was water in some type of aggression or accident, the test established, through the structure of the water, that it was literally 'poisoned' or 'dead'. In the North Pole, the researchers were left without water, so when they came to an ice floe – which was otherwise made of sea water, salty, and which was not for drinking – they prayed over the ice floe, and the water became as sweet as drinking water and thus saved them.

The human organism is about 75 per cent water. If the water receives information, it means that almost 75 per cent of the human organism receives information through different parts of the body linked to the brain. This suggests that the memory of water is in man – that is, the whole human organism records and remembers information through water – and that they are only processed in the brain. No source has the same water structure, and the composition is different in nuances. It was noted that before a person was born, if the mother was drinking water from a source area and the child was in the stomach and received information, if the person's life was taken away from the place of birth, he would always have the desire called 'nostalgia' to returns to the place from which he came.

Also, it was found that the structure of the cells of each person and that of the source of water in the place where he was born is exactly the same. By drinking water, a person enters the memory of that water and receives the information completely unconsciously because he himself is made of 75 percent water, and water remembers everything that is happening inside and around it, and it transmits the pathways of human consumption. All scientists who have been involved in and studying water claim that water has a 'photographic memory'.

Also, the abilities of races are different according to some nations. It's no coincidence that the most famous painters, sculptors, writers, composers, and scientists have come from a certain part of the world. The birth of great scientists has precisely determined the quality and structure of water in certain regions. The biggest wars today are precisely due to water, and in time, it will become the most expensive substance on the market.

There are special farms of fruits and vegetables, on which they are grown in special conditions and watered with pure spring water, uncoded water, the one that does not have information. Up to six times, the fruit and vegetables grow better in such conditions and have completely different flavours and smells than those grown on poor-quality soil, which is sprayed and watered with plain water, not seeing what that water carries in itself and from where it originates.

By consuming such fruits, people bring in all this information that can initiate different 'sick' conditions. People working in such high-quality farms pass the most stringent psychological and health tests, and even when they are not in a good mood that day, they are banned from working so as not to affect with their bad thoughts the energy of plants. So we bring in already stored water in the body, water that has experience and information in its memory field. From the source, while the water comes to the consumer, a series of procedures and chemical treatments are carried out for cleanliness, which disrupts its structure and is called 'dead water'.

We can wonder why there are no sick and obese animals. They eat natural food and drink natural spring water. Shodono bring health and strength to themselves by getting information about the nature they are in contact with. So we can list an example of a horse that will never drink water from a contaminated source. After oxygen, water is the most needed human compound. What is the synergy between man and water? The scientist Quinton came to the conclusion in 1887 that a human organism is analogous to sea water because it has exactly the same composition of minerals as blood plasma.

RTF: Human brain, water, artificial memory – is everything connected? Does everything have the possibility of memory, memorisation? What about plants and animals?

GSF: Many people are not aware that plants are complex organisms that live rich and sensual lives. Many see them as inanimate objects which do not differ much from the walls. The fact is that people can easily make flowers or artificial Christmas trees for a living, which is just an example of how they relate to plants. Dr Boris Holodenko worked on experiments with plants. He planted ten plants in one room, and in that room, a man who listened to classical music – Mozart, Beethoven, Bach – watered them with live spring water and directed to them words full of love, warmth, admiration. The plants responded in the same positive way as they were treated. They spread their leaves and looked healthy.

The next day, a man dressed in black with a very bad mood entered the same room with large scissors, approached five plants, and completely cut out their leaves, flowers, and stems. He threw everything cut to the floor, trampled on them, and behaved very aggressively. The other five plants were left untwisted, but their stems and leaves began to bend, the flowers too close. After a few days, the five plants treated with gentleness, love, and respect were revived and raised their leaves, the flowers and the nerves complete. Therefore, the plants remembered the person who had a positive attitude towards them and were very 'joyful' in responding. When the man in black who had been aggressive was there once again, the plants immediately began to bend their stems and leaves as if they were 'afraid'.

This experiment has proven that plants have memory as well as react by memory. They carry with them their own memory records, information received during cultivation – the quality of seeds, sowing, the people who feed them, the water they are watered with, and the sprayed pesticides. All this information enters our body, and this information goes into human memory, in a 'special file'.

Animals also have memory, and that memory really works. Animals can be dressed and trained and remember and store memory by the information through which their behaviour is manifested. We have the phenomenon of circus performances where various types of animals perform very complex stunts, both individually and together with other animals or humans. They also remember how people behave towards them, so people who are 'bad' to them are also remembered. It is known that elephants have a remarkable memory and that they are able to remember for decades and seek revenge.

The phenomenon of memory in elephants is the most pronounced and longest memory. All animals have the ability to store memory, but each type is different. Unlike humans, animals do not remember specific events, but instead, they can remember useful information that could help them survive. So dogs forget the event within two minutes, while chimps have a short-term memory of only twenty seconds.

The results of the latest study, in which twenty-five animals were tested, from pigeons to dolphins, showed that the average duration of short-term memory in animals was twenty-seven seconds. At the beginning of the experiment, a red circle was shown, and after a while, a black square appeared alongside it. An animal would receive a reward if it chose the form it had seen before a break, in this case a red circle.

The study shows that animals have different systems of short-term memory and special memories. And animals guard all the irritations in short-term memory, but this information disappears very quickly. They are able to preserve only some information that is, as a rule, extremely important for their survival. For example, the crows remember where they hid the nest even for several months, while most birds are not able to remember different information for more than a minute. Prof Joan Lind from the University of Stockholm said he was surprised by the poor results shown by chimpanzees since they are our closest relatives, and this discovery suggests that our memory capacity has significantly evolved.

I will cite some other examples. Rats often live in habitats near human settlements and can also be kept as pets. They are intelligent. They like to play with toys, and their behaviour is not the same as rats in the wild. They have a wide application in laboratory research, easily finding shortcuts and holes. A recent study has found that brown rats have awareness of their own thinking processes, which until now have been considered to be characteristic of only humans and some primates.

The octopus is perfectly adapted to the life of a hunter but also prey because it has a secret weapon. In its body, a black ink bag is released when it wants to confuse its enemies, and it can also drop a substance that blocks the sense of smell of the opponent so that it will not be able to find it. It has fantastic memory and can change the colour of its body to that of the seabed when it is suddenly scared. Pigeons are all around us, and most people view them as pests. However, these birds are actually quite smart. They are subjects of many scientific experiments. It is believed that pigeons were indoctrinated more than three thousand years before the new era. Past studies have shown that pigeons use the acquired experience and learn very quickly.

It is possible that forest animals adapt to life with humans, but when you return them to the forest, they will not forget the experience of what is outside of it. Squirrels have good memory and are cunning, which can help them escape from enemies. They have the ability to recognise their owners and show a certain learning ability because they know that they come to the call. Despite the reputation for fatigue and poor hygiene, pigs are actually very intelligent animals, even more intelligent than dogs. Their intelligence is measured by the intelligence of a child of 3 years. Because of the highly developed sense of smell, pigs are used to search for truffles in most European countries.

Some scientists believe that crows are more intelligent than primates. During the research, it was shown that the crows were intelligent enough to bend a piece of wire into a hook, which then served as a hook for catching worms sealed in an elongated plastic bowl. They are also known for throwing walnuts on a pedestrian crossing. The crows would wait patiently for some of the pedestrians to press the green light button and then, without danger, would gather their prey, which the car had previously smashed.

The first elephants appeared in Africa some twenty-three million years ago, when the horses dominated the herbivores. As a result of the struggle between elephants and horses for the same plant food, it happened that elephants had become larger through evolution. Elephants are known for using tools in different ways in the wild and can also follow human command in captivity. The incredible ability of elephants to learn and memorise shows that elephants have more brain cells per square centimetre than any other species of animals individually.

Orangutans live in widely scattered communities. The females remain with their young for years, teaching them everything they need to survive in the woods. They are seen using bathing sticks, fighting, or combing them. In captivity, they learned to open a closed box to get to the fruit that is in it. Tests have shown that they can communicate with people using simple sentences through symbolic panels.

Have you ever wondered why dolphins are the main attraction in most aquariums? This is because they are smarter than any other creature on the planet. They entered the water about fifty million years ago. They are exceptionally social animals and are known for their friendly attitude towards people, so they often approach them in the water with the indication that they want to play with them. Dolphins use the tools in their natural environment and can learn a variety of tricks and commands.

Chimps are the closest relatives of people and are genetically very close. According to the latest research, the hereditary material of chimps and humans coincides to about 98 per cent. Chimpanzees use different tools in search of food. They have developed a hunting strategy that requires mutual cooperation. They are also able to learn sign language and communicate with people. But perhaps the most unlikely characteristic of chimpanzees is their ability to use objects and symbols to convey their ideas.

RTS: Is there any evidence that the country is remembered? Did your research go in that direction?

GSF: Earth's surface is 75 per cent covered with water. In the earth's womb, there are also huge amounts of water, so as water has the ability to memorise, we can consider that all this quantity carries with it the potential of memory. Minerals, ores, crystals, metals – gold, silver, copper – silicon, and quartz are elements used to create artificial, digital, and nano-technology for computers, phones, and various other devices requiring memory. Artificial memory has recently been expanding its application in all branches of medicine to communication systems and to the simplest home watchmaker.

Still, Nikola Tesla claimed that there was the possibility of making artificial memory, which at the time was science fiction, but in time, the scientists would put it into practice, and artificial memory became available every day in various applications, from the home clock to the satellite. Planet Earth, from which minerals and other substances for the production of artificial memory are extracted, possesses the same in unlimited quantities, as well as water, which makes it capable of memory, so planet Earth is an inexhaustible source of information storage. With its memory capacity, the earth contains the same information from the very beginning, which also refers to the emergence of the human species and its evolution to the present. The earth is an infinite source of stored information, but we have not yet learned how to enter and read the earth's information field.

Very few genius people managed to touch the information field, and without knowing how to contact the field in special states of consciousness, they came up with information that provided epochal results. Among them are Plato, Nikola Tesla, Einstein, Leonardo Da Vinci, Nostradamus, etc., 'inspired' by the information that Jesus, Buddha, and so many other teachers who had their followers transmit from them in the form of messages and commandments. As we know, the earth is part of the universe and accordingly has the potentials of memory records from the universe and perfection. The earth is a part of the cosmos, with all its potentials and functions. Of whom? And why?

RTS: The memory of man, like his brain, is still largely a secret. How is all the information stored in man?

GSF: As we know, memory is a set of stored information, and the information itself is the thought, the feeling, the experience, and everything that is happening around us and within us. It is all information, but information and thoughts are intangible energies that do not function according to any known physical and material laws. There is a famous saying to the people – 'It's all been written down somewhere.' Man's memory is an information field that has a limit. Memory is not at all physically present in man, but it is energy that affects matter, as explained by memory processes in the brain.

A man does not die from the cessation of his heart, which has been proven to date by examples of clinical death. The death of a man occurs when the energy of information does not 'service' the brain and its functions, when the brain loses the energy of information. Then physical death occurs, and the energy of information, as energy that is indefensible, goes to the source and storage of the information field of the earth and the universe.

It is known to people that the soul never dies but moves. The soul is in fact a set of information both inherited and acquired during life. The energy of information does not work according to our conscious wishes or needs, although in special situations such as hypnosis regression, we can initiate and expand memory and get information from the distant past, which is not possible in a conscious state. This proves that a person in special, concentrated regressive states has a greater possibility of accessing memory records than those in the human memory source as well as in the memory records of the earth and the universe. Memory as information is energy that is not variable, not destructive and infinite.

All of us, until some time ago, lived with the thought that the thought is changeable, limited, and not part of the universe. However, the latest knowledge definitely confirms that thought is exactly the form of information energy that has no boundaries. Maybe this is not understandable to our previous knowledge but became one of the current topics of today's research, with the desire that a person fully understands the events around him and his untapped potentials and functions.

Phantom pain is permanent or occasional, blunt, irritating, glowing, or pulsating pain after amputation in an extremity that is missing. It is amplified by changes in time and emotional stress. In about 80 per cent of cases, after the amputation, there is a sense of phantom extremity – that is, a situation in which the patient seems to have an amputated limb still present. Patients feel touch, warmth, or cold, even the position in which the extremity is located. Sometimes it seems to them that the missing limb is more severe than the other, or they have the so-called telescopic feeling, where it seems to them that the amputated extremity becomes shorter over time. In rare cases, there is pain in a non-existent extremity. The mechanism of phantom pain has not been fully clarified.

It is evident that phantom pain works in these 80 per cent of people, while the pain of the 20 per cent is suppressed in the subconscious and remains as a memory. A cumulative memory of the removed organ or extremity remains in the memory field. It is not erasable and manifests itself in consciousness or subconsciousness. The memory energy that is written is indestructible and infinite.

The phenomenon of children with innate physical anomalies or the lack of some extremities or organs do not coincide with the phenomenon of phantom pain because they are born without limbs or organs and with birth do not have a record, either inborn or not acquired, of the presence of that limb or organ. The phenomenon of phantom pain shows us that the disappearance of the physical body does not disappear from the memory of a complete person. That is, when the physical body of a man ceases to function fully, dies, the energy of information about him, the soul, does not disappear but remains in the memory field of the earth and the whole universe.

I'll explain something more. In cases of organ transplantation, the transplanted organ appears to be accepted or discarded. The previous belief is that 'the body has not accepted the organ'. However, this theory is not entirely true. The transplanted organ has its own characteristics and certain frequencies, 'vibrations' of the donor. If the energy of communication of the brain, the main energy centre of a person, is not realised, then the transplanted organ does not execute the orders given to it and is rejected via organ smothering. This is an explanation of why, in fact, the body will not accept it.

However, in cases when the organ is accepted, communication between the brain and the transplanted organ occurs in patients. The most frequent cases of 'accepted' organs are between parents and children, brothers and sisters, as well as among close relatives, and this is because they function at the same frequencies of information transmission. It is customary to attribute this success to tissue matching. Nevertheless, they also have information that is genetically encoded, i.e. information that is transmitted or 'typed' from generation to generation.

12

Two Main Manifestations

RTS: What is your opinion on the experience of many people who claim to have had so-called meetings with people who 'come from another time'?

GSF: My personal opinion is that these are the kinds of confessions of people who have really experienced such experiences. Unfortunately, there were also a large number of those who wanted to draw the attention of the environment or the general public to themselves, summarising some experiences based on imagination or phantasmagoria. It's about mentally lazy or beneficial people who have greatly doubted that such things are happening anyway.

There were also those who tried to convince others of the experience but in a very clumsy way, bringing even more confusion. However, in a number of cases, careful examination has determined that these are true events – that is, that people really had experiences that they describe very often in detail. Unfortunately, I must note that there were such cases that people with such claims were sent to mental hospitals and diagnosed with schizophrenia and the like because people simply did not believe them and were not able to check or investigate such occurrences.

RTS: Are these so-called visionary people 'hypersensitive' or 'psychics'?

GSF: No, it's not about people who claim to belong to any of these categories. In all the cases I have encountered in practice, it's about 'ordinary' people who have never had similar experiences before or simply were not aware of them. Among them are people who deal with scientific work, doctors, highly educated people, as well as people of very average education of different ages.

Almost everyone had one kind of fear and discomfort at the beginning of our conversation. They knew that their experiences were indeed survived, but they were afraid that they would come to understand them and what explanation would come to be for what they had experienced. You know, people are afraid that because of this experience, they can be declared untrustworthy, crazy, sick. Even though their experience has left a very striking sense of mingling with fear, suspicion, experience, sometimes material evidence, one part of their being is still wondering if what they had experienced really happened.

Knowing this, I had to often encourage them with a laugh. 'Only the lunatic claims that everyone around him is a mad man and that he is the only normal one.' In addition, bearing in mind that everyone is coming with the recommendation of their doctor to determine how the 'third type' is encountered, with some explanations of my approach to this 'problem' to ascertain more facts about the phenomenon with which they met, I managed to tear down the barrier they set themselves.

RTS: Can you explain to us what this is about, and how does it happen?

GSF: At the very outset, I emphasise that these are very serious things and that I also devoted considerable attention to this by researching and documenting cases but also those with which I am sure of my practice. I admit that at the beginning, I was very suspicious of everything I had had the opportunity to hear about or read. For many of the photos they provided to me, I was inclined to believe that it was a montage rather than a credible photo.

However, as time passed, I was sure that there was something else that surpassed previous experiences in medicine and science in general. I could not explain to myself how this does not happen to everyone but only some of us. The appearance of so-called ghosts always caused great attention and controversial claims. But when you find a person who describes everything in detail to you, takes a photo which you submit to forensics to determine its credibility, and when you find that this is a real experience based on material evidence, then it really matters for you to think and further research on such phenomena.

After analysing several cases with which I had the opportunity to meet in my practice, I found that in each of these events, there was a kind of 'trigger' for such a manifestation. To say so, 'conditions' or 'open doors' have been created for such an experience.

RTS: Can you explain to us more about how this is happening?

GSF: This type of phenomenon has not been determined in science and in medical practice. I call them two-time events. Why? Because I am absolutely sure that in all cases, it is about 'breaking' time frames – that is, overlapping and compression in a certain space. I now responsibly claim, after my experience and research, that many, at first glance, 'supernatural' phenomena experienced by individuals or groups of people are actually the result of similar misinterpretations and that the essence of the problem lies precisely in the paradox of time.

Although everything works intricately, there is an explanation. Those who do not want or cannot accept this will remain forever deprived of information that can provide them with answers to many questions in their lives. As I already mentioned, I myself initially fell into that trap, but I got rid of it with perseverance and searching for answers to the questions that tormented me.

Do not mind that I give this introduction to this whole story – which, in my opinion, requires a lot of explanation – before I go through concrete examples from practice. I consider this to be necessary precisely because such events do not happen to everyone so obviously, or many of us simply do not register them. I emphasise that almost nothing is the same in our environment as it seems to us to be or how it is presented to us. We see different events and claim that one happened before the other. We give them a timetable. We measure this by various timers of thinking that we measure between two or more events.

And can we always say with certainty that something really happened and exactly at what time? This is a key question. If two or more events were at a certain distance from us and each other, information about them comes at different times, and we are not aware of it. Someone who watches them from another place can come to the conclusion that they happened at the same time or they claim to be completely opposite to us.

Our senses are based on the reception of information carried by an information broker, and it can often be 'distorted'. By involving more senses in the process of receiving various information, the situation becomes even more complicated, as is the case with those associated with light or sound. For example, we first see the light, and then we hear the thunder. An ankle hammer blow is often heard with a slight delay in relation to the moment of contact of the hammer to the anvil. All this entails confusion in the complete processing of the information we collect through the senses.

RTS: Is it the case when it comes to time and space?

GSF: The difference between time and space, which I have already mentioned before, has long been established, based on the fact that space itself seems to us a whole, time as something that flows through some of its 'dosed' pace and measured by various timers – digital, mechanical, sand, or other instruments.

Time is divided into the past, the present, and the future. We went through the analysis by 'remembering' the past, 'living' in the present, or 'looking at the side' or 'forecasting or planning' the future. In spite of the fact that it is possible for today's man to determine or measure less time units for the devices made for it, it is difficult to determine what is the present – that is, when it begins and when it is exactly done.

Modern physics, as a scientific discipline, has adopted the philosophical idea of the universal reality, while on the other hand, we have everything that moves in the universe of unspecified direction and the exact speed of movement. It is hard for a man to accept that all the parameters determining his existence are, in fact, vague except for time. Although most of us still view time as a thread that runs between two points – birth and death.

Imagery about a dimension that cannot be mathematically expressed or acquired by sight is difficult to accept. Man does not think of the present as the past or the future because it is unnatural to him. Space and time are a continuum. For this reason, it is impossible to draw a clear boundary in what we call the past or the future or the present. Why did I mention the continuum? Because in the biological sense, the fourth dimension is, in fact, continuity.

For example, in the tomb of an Egyptian pharaoh, grain cereals, after almost four thousand years, are clinging and stacked in a stalk and do not differ from the grain that emerged just four years ago from the seeds of the same sown along the Nile's trough. What does that tell us? This clearly indicates that life is winning the distance of even four thousand years. It's similar to space because you should remember that everything is in the eye of the spectators and in the individual experience of the world around us.

Kozir and Mjuzes had 'different' views of the energy of time, claiming that time had its own form of energy. They have not fully approached their claims and theories with the 'acceptable' explanation of the social and scientific public, and to this day, we are wandering about the synthesis of time and space or need an explanation for certain manifestations that are happening around us, and we only record them, each in its own way, in the form of information. In contemporary science, the following formulas for time and movement are completely accepted:

Straight linear motion

v = (speed); $s = v \cdot t$ (travelled path); $t = s / v$ (time)

If we stop to observe time and movement as a straight phenomenon, these formulas immediately 'fall into the water'. Now we come to the question 'How can we then make calculations and interpret the occurrences of movement in space and time?' The most accurate answer to this question is a budget based on the possibility of a reverse process in which matter affects time. This means that nothing happens without certain consequences or manifestations because we live in the continuum of space and time.

Two scientists who have attracted the most attention by dealing with the issue of space and time are, of course, Newton and Einstein. I would not deal with the analysis of their claims and 'random errors' now, but I will say that in addition to Maxwell and Tesla, in the theoretical as well as experimental sense, they were closest to the explanation of two-time events. The following figure shows the view of time dimensions in more detail:

Depending on the number of 'space' dimensions, the distance between the two points is determined in different ways. In the one-dimensional space, the length of the OA is only the distance along the x-axis, and this measurement is trivial easily. For the 2-D space, the length of the longer OA is determined by the famous Pythagorean theorem:

$$(\; OA = \sqrt{x^2 + y^2} \;)$$

In 3-D, the theorem is expanding and still valid.

$$OA = \sqrt{x^2 + y^2 + z^2}$$

After STR showed that the distance along with time must be calculated, determining the exact equation was no longer an easy task. Mathematics that includes all known laws for 2-D that make geometry and trigonometry at the level of development is over a long period. These laws are gradually expanded to three dimensions, and they are in the branches of mathematics called spherical trigonometry and geometry in space. However, these branches of mathematics could not 'win a battle' with an additional time factor, so a completely new branch of mathematics had to be developed, a so-called tensor account to include this factor. In this way, a space–time distance formula appeared, its final form the following:

In the above equation, c denotes the speed of light and t time. When it was recognised that this term is similar to the Pythagorean theorem with the addition of two factors (c and t), it has been concluded that time behaves as if it is the fourth dimension, thus the discussion about the space–time continuum.

The basis of Einstein's general theory of relativity is that gravity curves in four dimensions in the space–time continuum. Of course, for the visual representation of a four-dimensional space–time continuum, the principles have reached a consensus for the claim that 'superhuman ability' is needed, which, in my opinion, is superfluous as the experience of some people speaks the opposite.

Documentary evidence in photographs, videos, and statements of people undergoing deep hypnosis also indicate the existence of two-time manifestations and their frequency. Numerous examples are already known to a wider circle of those dealing with this and similar issues, and I would not quote them on this occasion. Anyone who is a little more interested can already find them in some publications or the internet. For them, I cannot guarantee 100 per cent authenticity, but it is very likely that they are credible, I can say.

RTS: Now that it's clearer what two-time manifestations are and how they come about, can you give us some specific cases with which you had the opportunity to meet them?

GSF: The code of ethics, even the law, does not allow me to discover the true identity of the person who had this experience and with whom I investigated the causes and manifestations of such a phenomenon. Bearing in mind that it is important that as many people share their experience of the two-time events that have been tested for special forensic methods that have really happened, I asked them to write them down as much as possible and give me the approval to publish them using initials or pseudonyms instead of their real names. Of course, I know these people, and to a large extent, I can thank them for having achieved mutual trust, which has resulted in truly new valuable knowledge of our reality.

Here is one of those testimonies of the person, who was, at that moment, 19 years old. It is a law student from Serbia, a completely psychologically and physically healthy person of the male sex, expressing intelligence and a rational way of thinking. I would ask those who read this to read each sentence carefully because it is very important to get acquainted with a person who had such an experience to feel what it is actually about.

'I was sitting on the bed in my room after I had just finished the work that I had with my colleague working for the Roman Law exam. It was necessary for my colleague and I to make a table in the largest format with the laws and their donors according to the chronological order of adoption. I put a white hammer on the wall of my room and watched her sitting on the bed. I took my mobile phone to paint it and sent my fellow the picture. I took a photo.

'She was kind of "blurry" when I wanted to see her fall out. Although my mobile phone takes extremely good photos, I made another one from almost the same position. She was better, and I sent her the picture with a comment that the job was done. I went back to the previous photo in an attempt to delete it so that I did not take up space in the phone's memory. I was wondering why it was blurred. I zoomed in and was scared.

'In disbelief, I saw the photo I had recorded with my mobile phone and watched simultaneously in my room the area where the photo was taken. There was a "person" I did not see, but it was recorded by my mobile phone camera. It was about eleven o'clock in the morning, and there was completely natural light in my room. I was very scared by the fact that somebody was present in my immediate vicinity and that I could not see him with my own eyes.

'My parents were out of the house. I immediately asked them to come. I felt fear. I sent them a photo for them to see. I did not notice anything about or moving around the room, nor did I notice anything unusual happening. Still, I did not like what I saw on the photo. I no longer wanted to be alone in the house, alone in my room, where I had spent most of my time ever since my earliest childhood and in which all things had been known to me so far.'

It is clearly visible, the person about whom the young man speaks. With the image enlarged, this is even better seen. In the photo on the right, in the upper left corner, you can see a part of the 'halo', which means that it is nothing but the orb of huge dimensions that carries information in it, while the figure of soldier in the painting that we have magnified makes it easier to explain.

What can be clearly concluded, even to a layman, is that this should be 'mounted' to make it credible as the man in the military uniform in the left part of the photo, in '3-D' mode – by the bookshelf on which sits a monitor and a glass table – is partially reflected as well as other things that are in the immediate vicinity. The hologram display turned off the forensics as well as the possibility that anything was 'mounted'. I had an insight into that report provided by my mother's boyfriend. For me, this was nothing new and weird because I had had the opportunity to see it before. Analysing the photo, I came to the fact that the uniform was worn by a soldier from a photo from the Second World War.

So it's a time distance of about eighty years. The 'trigger' was the young man's focus on Roman law – that is, laws, court proceedings, and the like. It is possible that the person in the picture is innocently or unfairly condemned and 'searches for justice' in the continuum of time, which is often the case with various cases of 'ghost display', characterised as science fiction stories.

RTS: You mentioned 'ghosts'. Is this a common name for people who have lived in 'past times' and appear in the 'present'?

GSF: I would say that with cyclical patterns of life. This is materialised evidence of two-time phenomena that indicate that matter is indestructible and that it is possible to 'travel' through space and time, disappearing and appearing cyclically according to 'triggers' from the outside environment. Every living organic matter has the ability to reproduce. It moves from dimension to dimension, embodies it according to the same form it was created as.

The ancient Greeks still recorded their claims about metamorphosis – the relocation of the soul into a new body – and similar beliefs were also found in ancient nations, even ancient civilisations. So far, there has been much evidence that the soul has come to be misunderstood, but as long as knowledge of other places and time is attributed only to those who live 'now and here' or those who are still alive, in relative time and space, we will wander into the hallways of ignorance.

It is not necessary that 'ghosts' appear in bodily shape. The phenomenon of their occurrence in different times and spaces, owing to two-time manifestations, can be viewed in the context of 'astral projection'. Of course, it's about a 'supernatural' process that is very common. Many claim to have seen a person who 'suddenly disappeared' from the sight, do they not?

On the other hand, it is not uncommon to claim that they talked to a person they knew while being 'alive' and that they had an uncomfortable meeting again with that person and led the conversation as if they were 'alive again' and in the immediate vicinity of very clear display and speech. Particularly for 'ghosts', they almost always move to places where they lived and 'during their lifetime'. There is no question about spiritism, the invocation of the dead. This is about their appearance without the desire or provoking their presence.

RTS: Are there any earlier research attempts to explain these phenomena?

GSF: In that direction, research by Konstantīns Raudive, a psychologist who had discovered tape recordings during conversations with people who spoke directly into a microphone full of quiet foreign voices, were also moving. By connecting a tape recorder with a set of crystal diodes and a very short antenna, it has been found that these voices speak in strange languages, like Esperanto, in strange rhythms but that they coincide with an interval that answers what seems to fit his asked questions.

The presence of votes has been recorded on tape recorders, and there is no doubt in their existence. This process has been investigated and analysed by many scientists who have examined the equipment used and listened to the tapes. Raudive argues that a man 'carries with him the ability to contact his [living] friends after leaving this world'. In other words, he believes that voices belong to the dead.

A man is not yet sufficiently familiar with the self nor with the world surrounding him. To the maximum extent, ignorance and suspicion are factors that limit him from activating the 'sixth sense' or from the state of active search for information through the received code. We rely too heavily on the senses that we have, to say so, limited possibilities. The process of receiving, processing, and storing data takes place in the human brain. If we take into account that only part of the human brain is in the status of actively processing this data, we come to the conclusion that for the rest of the brain that is unknown, we are waiting for an answer, or the answer is there, only we have not recognised it.

One thing is certain, however, and I categorically assert this – two-time manifestations are a common phenomenon that is initiated by stimuli from an environment of one dimension and transferred to another without a space and time limit.

RTS: Do you know that there are photographs that have covered the imagination of those open minds and triggered an avalanche of questions about what you call 'two-way events'?

GSF: Yes, these are the photographs that have been seen by the world in search of the right answer to the questions 'Is it possible?' and 'Does it really happen?' External stimulations can initiate such phenomena, such as the appearance of one person in 'more places' or 'different times'. One of these photographs is the next, where we see that a girl, whom the photographers called 'a phantom girl', appears on several different photos, painted in a completely different time and in a different place.

Just using new technologies and zooming in on yellowed images made for decades or more before the Bolshevik Revolution of 1917, one could clearly see it on many photographs. The Regional Museum of Local

Heritage in Krasnoyarsk has launched an investigation into the identity of the girl, who is believed to have been between eight and ten years old when the photographs were made.

[Photo: Krasnoyarsk Regional Museum of Local Lore / siberiantimes.com]

One of the most striking photographs shows her posing on a roof in front of the famous Railway Bridge in Krasnoyarsk, which opened in 1899 and through which the Trans-Siberian Railway crosses the Yenisei River. Despite the well-kept documentation and archives of local photographers of that time, researchers are not able to determine who had painted the 'Phantom Girl', as they called her. Local experts estimated that the pictures originated from the period from 1906 to 1908 but insist that the photographs were not made during one painting on the same day.

RTS: Can you explain to us more about how this kind of phenomenon arises?

GSF: Information has its own self. It is timeless and ubiquitous. People in some way had experiences with that person, that at one moment, the thought of someone was invoked by that person, and the appearance of that person at that moment was very intense. Everything was circumspectly and timely on these photographs. This is the so-called 'trigger' – goggles of invisible information recorded by cameras or technical devices that can store information in a moment.

Man has no thoughts but the ability to collect information. This information is overlapped at one point, and such documents are created in the form of photographs, videos, sound. Do not forget – information is indestructible. It has the characteristic of the current concept of teleportation, which is also evident in the example of the next photo that shows one and the same woman who, even on the black-and-white photograph, has the same coloured attire that the participants of the recorded photograph claim to have not seen at all by the naked eye.

I will mention another example known as the 'Spirit of Freddy Jackson'. Namely, this photo was taken in 1919 and was first published by Sir Victor Goddard, a retired RAF colonel in 1975. The photo is a group portrait of the Goddard Squadron, which served in the First World War on the ship HMS *Dedal*. In the photo, there was the freaky face of Freddy Jackson, a mechanic who was accidentally killed by a plane propeller two days before the photo was painted. His assassination was held exactly the day when the group portrait was painted, and all members of the squadron easily recognised his face.

Although the photo has been published for many years, the image remains a mystery as no one has successfully proved 'manipulation'. It is completely clear here that this is a two-time event. Through the code, we get information from the 'past' and 'future'. I am talking about time inversion, which I defined with the following formula:

$I \times Vn\ (F)$
$T \pm 1$
Km — collective memory
I — information
T — weather
Vn (F) — vector space

To put it simply, these phenomena occur when two times overlap at one point or when information is teleported from one vector space from collective memory over time. These phenomena are constantly happening.

RTS: On the synthesis of matter and information, what do you consider as the cost?

GSF: So timeless and omnipresent information is manifested continuously, as evidenced by the described cases recorded with the camera which we had explained. The information is indestructible and ubiquitous. It does not lose its intensity, but it is constantly increasing. The synthesis of the spirit, matter, and information represents a *cost* which is manifested through a series of characteristic, unique forms, whose appearance is independent of time and space.

I will also note that the soul, as a kind of energy, exists independently of the body but has always been misinterpreted among the scientific public as well as in scientific information. The evidence for this claim is, among other things, these photographs as well as many other aspects of the phenomena that classical science puts aside, masquerading with superficial and often inaccurate interpretations, mystifying and blurring a true view of our reality. Especially when it comes to the 'deceased' people who appear – that is, in the real-time realm after their deaths – science has no answer.

The answer to this question is exactly the explanation I have given – information about anything to anyone who can manifest everywhere and everywhere because the information is indestructible, and so is the 'record' of people who have 'completed their earthly lives'. Their appearance is recorded in individual moments, and we call this phenomenon two-way manifestations.

RTS: Is there at least one indication, at least one piece of information in modern science, that points us in that direction?

GSF: Science so far had no explanation regarding these phenomena, or these explanations were completely divergent. People generally accepted these explanations because it was imposed on them as 'true' and the 'only' proof. What I claim is purely based on tangible evidence of what is happening in the process of biennial manifestations, and there is no more place for 'free scientific interpretations'. Two-way events are our reality. Face that truth and accept it as part of yourself. This is the truth that happens to us in everyday life. There is no other truth.

13

Information and Its Energy Field

RTS: First of all, what should be information in your opinion?

GSF: There is a large number of universally accepted definitions that attempt to figure out what information is, how man uses it, and what its significance is for man in general terms.

At the beginning, I would like to point out that I have seen all available interpretations of the notion of information. With some, I could have somehow agreed, but their essence is debatable for me. To better understand what information is or, rather, how information is presented to us, we will make a small retrospective of the current 'knowledge set' about information, from etymology to given definitions. In support of this, we will also include some of the definitions that are most common in the field that we call 'official science' or, if you want, 'public opinion'.

Information is a Latin word. It originally means 'putting in a certain form' – that is, giving shapes to something. However, it lost its original meaning over time. Information – abbreviated as *info* – is what oe informs, i.e. the one from which it will be derived. Information is provided either as messages or through direct or indirect observation of something. What is most important is for it to be construed as a message in its own right, and in that sense, information is always transmitted as the content of the message. The information can be encoded in different forms for the transmission of the interaction.

For example, information can be encoded by remnants and transferred to a destination. The English word is derived from *informative*. The noun is derived from the Latin *informare*, 'inform', with the meaning 'give form to the mind', 'discipline', 'teach', 'lecture'. *Info* comes from, through the French *informer*, the Latin verb *informare*, which means to give shape or formulate an idea. In addition, the Latin term itself has already contained the recombination with the meaning of a concept or idea, although the extent to which it influenced the development of word formation in English is not clear.

The old Greek word μορφή (*morf*) and tudiεῖδος (*eidos*) mean 'type, idea, form, set'. A later word is known for its use by Plato – and later Aristotle – in a technical, philosophical sense to denote an ideal identity or the essence of something, a form of view. *Eidos* can also be related to thought, suggestion, or even concept. The ancient Greek for information translates *plērophoria* to πλήρης (*plērēs*) and φέρω (*phorein*). This literally means 'completely relates' or 'transmissions in full'.

In modern Greek, the word Πληροφορία is still in daily use and has the same meaning as 'recombination' in English. Unfortunately, biblical scholars have translated *plērophoria* as 'complete confidence' by creating the connotational meaning of the word. In addition to its primary meaning, the word Πληροφορία has deep roots in the Aristotelian triangle. In that respect, it can be interpreted to communicate the information of one decoding of a specific type of character.

This is something that often happens with the etymology of many words in ancient and modern Greek when there is a very strong denotative relationship between the signifier meaning, e.g. the word symbol that declares a specific encoded interpretation, and the marked, e.g. the concept whose meaning the interpreter is trying to decode. With the concepts of communication, we will deal with the most diverse situations, from the use in everyday life to those in specialised scientific fields. It is a basic feature of the modern so-called Information Age, information science, and technology.

From the many meanings it possesses, this section deals with the aspect of information that connects with the concept of the message. Since data information is often used as synonyms, it is important to make distinctions among them. Namely, the definition of information reads that some data is placed in a meaningful context, while other data is out of context. In other words, the data is useless until it transmits some information.

According to the following definition, information is a set of signs that mean something to the recipient, who discovers something new. *Information* is a term with many meanings depending on the context, but as a rule, it is narrowed down to concepts such as meaning, knowledge, perception, instruction, communication, and various processes.

Simply put, information and its message are received. But first of all, it is the result of processing, manipulating, and organising data in a way that they upgrade the knowledge of the person receiving the information. Communication theory is a numerical representation of the uncertainty of outcomes. We associate with the *sentropium* of information and therefore with the relevance of the message, i.e. how much information was given to us. On the other hand, the message is a materialised form of information. The main characteristic of the message is that it is informative – that is, it provides some new information to the one to whom it is intended, the recipient. Information is always about something, and in this sense, it can be false or true.

To be as pertinent and more meaningful, it is important that all participants in the communication channel have a certain knowledge about the given matter. Although the theory also deals with models that, along with the recipient, necessarily imply the existence of a sender and therefore do not attach importance to the idea that information can arise from the environment, it should be noted that the information and message must not be viewed in a strictly linguistic context, for even the noise that impedes the flow of communication gives some information.

Often information can be viewed as the type of input of the organisational system. There are two types of inputs. Some entries are inherently important for the functioning of an organism, e.g. food, or systems, e.g. energy. In his popular book *Sensory Ecology*, Dusenbery calls them causal entrances. Other inputs of information are important only because they are related to causative inputs and can be used to predict the occurrence of causative inputs in the future or perhaps somewhere else.

Some information is important because it is related to other information, although there must finally be a link to the causal input. In practice, information is usually transmitted through poor stimuli that must be detected through specialised sensory systems and enhanced by input energy before they become functional for an organism or system.

For example, light is often the causative input of plants, while it provides information to animals. Colourful light reflected from the flower is too weak to carry out significant photosynthetic work, while the bee's visual system detects it, and the bee's nervous system uses this information to guide the flower, where the bee often finds nectar or pollen, causal entrances that have a nutritional function.

Information is any type of form that influences the formation or transformation of other patterns. In this sense, there is no need for a conscious mind to see and even under-appreciate patterns. An example is

DNK. Sequential acute paternity affects the formation and development of an organism without the need for a conscious mind. System theory sometimes appears to refer to individual information in that sense, assuming that information is not necessary to include the conscious mind, and the circulating circles of persons, retorts, in the system can be called information.

In other words, it can be said that information, in this sense, is something potentially perceived as a representation, although it has not been created or presented for this purpose. For example, Gregory Bates defines information as 'a change that makes a difference'. If, however, the presumption of 'influence' implies that the information has been recognised and consciously interpreted by the mind, the specific context associated with that interpretation may cause the information to be transformed. The complex definitions of *information* and *knowledge* make such semantic and logical analysis difficult, although the condition of 'transformation' is an important point in the study of information as it relates to knowledge, especially in the business discipline of knowledge management.

In this practice, tools and specific processes are used that help the information expert carry out research and decision making, including steps such as reviewing information to effectively capture individual values and/or individual meanings, referencing the data, if available, establishing a relevant context, often selected among many possible contexts, carrying out new knowledge from information, and making decisions or recommendations, resulting in knowledge.

Some modern theorists claim that the transformation of information into knowledge is critical, that it lies at the core of the value of creating even competitive companies. The Danish dictionary of information states that information only provides an answer to the question asked. Whether the answer provides knowledge depends on the informed person. Therefore, the general definition of the concept should be 'information equals answers to specific questions'.

I will give another example, i.e. the interpretation of information. In the case when philosopher and enlightener Marshall McLuhan mediates its influence on human cultures, he talks about the structure of the various kinds that shape our behaviour and way of thinking. Also, the Spheromone often says that 'information' is in that sense. From the angle of an average educated man, the information represents every bit of knowledge of something that perceptively can be adopted and interpreted. Much information simply 'escapes' our senses, even if we are not aware of its existence or the form in which it manifests itself.

RTS: How do you interpret information from the angle of entropy?

GSF: Entropy represents the measure of average information content by the symbol of a source that represents a system or an information sequence. In the theory of information, as a measure of the amount of information in a message, it can serve as much as the change in the probability of the event occurring under the influence of that message. For example, if the summer weather forecast for tomorrow is 30°C, this will not bring us much information because it does not contain anything unexpected. However, if the same forecast occurs in winter, it is completely unexpected news and therefore contains a lot of information.

Information can also be considered a measure of remedied uncertainty. The more symbols we receive from sources, the more we get more information and insecurity drops over what could be sent. So far, many theorists have tried to clarify the definition of information from several aspects, but this is not so simple. Information has certain content – that is a fact – but each of us interprets that content in our own way.

In the theory of information, entropies of uncertainty are associated with a random variable. In this context, it is commonly referred to as Shannon entropy, which quantifies the expected value of the information contained in the message, usually in units such as being. Equally, Shannon's entropy is a measure of the average informational content that is leaked when the value of a random variable is not known. The concept introduced Claude Shannon to his famous work from 1948, *Mathematical Theory of Communications*.

You know that one coin turn wears an entropy of one bit. Two throws equals two bits. The rate of entropy for the coin is one bit after throwing. However, if the coin is not fair, then uncertainty is less – if we had to bet on the outcome of the next attempt, we would probably bet on a more frequent result – so Shannon's entropy is smaller. Mathematically, one throw of the coin, whether fair or not, is the Bernoulli experiment, but its entropy is given by a binary entropy function. A series of throwing a coin with two heads will have zero entropy as the outcomes are completely predictable. The speed of English text entropy is from 1 to 1.5 bits per letter or from 0.6 to 1.3 bits per letter, based on experiment-based estimates.

RTS: How many laws of entropy that we know explain the process of creating and exchanging information in relation to what really happens in our own, as we call it, practice?

GSF: Every event in the world is unique. For this reason, it is impossible to assert future events with certainty. Most of all, science can, in this field, based on observations, determine the likely scenario of future events. The famous anthropologist Max Gluckman once gave an opinion on human knowledge and science, describing it as a discipline in which 'the stupid generation of this generation can outweigh the level reached by the genius in the previous generation'.

I often thought about that claim. Yes, it is true if we exclude spirituality and put everything into the context of the material. The total content of knowledge, information, and science, if you so desire, is constantly increasing, but the total energy content circulating in the cosmos is unchanged. Thus, entropy is constantly increasing, while energy is constant, and it is impossible to destroy it or create it. It exists. It is given by the Creator.

We can only influence, in part, its shape or transformation – that is, how it will manifest at a certain time in a certain space. So we can direct and partially change the form of energy and in no way create or destroy it. An example of this is almost the whole of Tesla's work. Since information is nothing but energy, the same holds true for it. We cannot create or destroy it, just use it or shape it.

Rudolf Clausius, who had introduced the concept of entropy, argued that in a closed system, the difference in energy levels always strives to be equalised. On the second law of thermodynamics, he concludes that entropy in the world always tends to be maximised. The essence is that it is not enough to understand the law of entropy. It also needs to be experienced, felt. We need to know that energy is the foundation of life.

For this reason, the power in society belongs to the one who has power over the exosomatic instruments used for the exchange, transformation, and storage of energy. Many anthropologists have already noticed this, pointing out that the energy background of a particular environment is the basic determinant in shaping civilisation. But one should keep in mind that we can use free will in determining the speed at which the process of entropy takes place, i.e. whether it accelerates or slows down. Only in this way can a person somewhat control the laws and processes of entropy – that is, energy.

RTS: Are you aware of the fact that anyone in the world, apart from scientists or researchers, is thinking this way?

GSF: I believe that there are those who observe but do not research and that there are also those who are researching, but they do not dare to share the facts with others for known reasons. You know, for a long time, this was all a secret for a man. Do not ask me why. Just recently, as a signal, information, or input from the Creator, there begins to 'gather' a group that shares similar thoughts and is not afraid to say them out loud and share them with the rest of the world.

Investigating, I came to the conclusion that others are similarly thinking or coming to the same conclusions. I found the parallels of my research with other scientists in the world. Namely, one of those whose published research is almost identical to mine is also an academic, the head of the Neurosurgery Department of the Centre for Neurology and Neurosurgery, RNPC, neurosurgeon Arnold Fjedorovic Smjejanovic, with over forty-seven years of practice. During his career, he performed a large number of brain surgeries in almost nine thousand patients. Yet this man claims that the human brain is 99.9 per cent secret for us! I will quote one part of his interview that he recently gave.

'Yes, I see in front of myself a substance, cells that are filled with so much scope of knowledge that I want, like Newton, to take off the cap before every research. It's not clear how he works. For each nervous or eye signal, a "picture" is created in it. As a result, the person realises that it is a monkey, that it is a lamp. It is clear that the brain is more powerful than any supercomputer. Such processor frequencies are measured by gigahertz and terahertz, and man has only kilohertz. The signal does not go from a neuron to a neuron at a speed of light but 1,400 metres per second. However, the brain "works" much faster. The most surprising is that consciousness has no place in the body, but there is a connection of the brain and thoughts, which is a great secret. It is ruled by, probably, the Creator.'

Academician Smjejanovic claims that the brain does not produce thought but only processes it. There are other scientists who have seriously dealt with this topic and made their views public. Academician of the Russian Academy of Sciences and the Academy of Medical Sciences Natalya Behtereva admitted that when she and her staff tried to understand deep brain structures – for the first time in the USSR, scientists used the method of long-term implantation of electrodes – they immediately got sick. They felt so bad that they did not have the strength for any research. It was enough to stop the experiment. Power and health returned to them immediately.

The winner of two state awards of the USSR, a surgeon of Sveti, Luka Vojno Jasenecki, compared the brain to telephone exchange, whose role is reduced to giving a statement. It does not add anything to what it gets. Nobel Prize winner for physiology and medicine John Eckles, who had discovered the ionic mechanism of initiation and inhibition in peripheral and central nervous cells, believed that the brain does not 'produce' thoughts but receives it from the outside.

An extraordinary woman, Behtereva was not afraid of devastating, humiliating criticism from her colleague, a materialist. She said that the human brain is able to create only simple thoughts. Where are theories, hypotheses, discoveries born? It is still unknown to physiologists. I am also convinced that the human brain is one big enigma – the universe in the human organism, one big secret whose part we have yet to discover.

RTS: Your research gives a completely new theory or a new view of information. Do you have the desire to share it with the rest of mankind?

GSF: I have, and I'm not afraid of what the 'official science' will say about it, of the individuals or groups that may not agree with it. I've never felt that sort of fear, which I think is pointless. I accept responsibility not to be confused by everything I say, and I am ready to prove it at any time. It would be self-centred to come to some knowledge and to keep it for itself. Why then?

Of course, there are 'secrets' that are shared only with 'selected ones', but these are the cases when you estimate it is the best, and the time shows if you were right or wrong. Namely, the existing definitions of information do not fully define information. Most often, as we have seen, these definitions say that it is a set of data about someone and/ or something. Information is an intangible energy-related substance. It's about energy that cannot be destroyed. Information is omnipresent energy that has the ability to transform from one form to another regardless of space and time. It has the characteristics of unspoken movement in time and space – a kind of teleportation. A man is able to recognise these characteristics, but he is often unaware of it. At the same time, it remains with the laptop and the one who receives it.

Therefore, it is constantly multiplying. One example is NASA, which sends signals to the cosmos to establish communication with other intelligences, and this information is constantly circulating. Information that is broadcast in the air is indestructible. Its transformation is somewhat possible, but it cannot be destroyed. Human life is created and takes place on the principles of information. It is the most powerful energy on our planet and probably in the cosmos. Our DNA is nothing but a chain of information with the possibility of transformation.

I want to draw attention to the fact that the term *collectively unconscious* is wrong. It's collective memory with an unknown capacity. One piece we want to 'extract' can be achieved by regression, the third degree of the alpha status, but I would like to do so later. We also come to the question of what constitutes an information memory field or COD. Collective memory is not available to everyone but only individual codes for its recognition. A huge number of those who pretend to be 'visionary' are limited by a combination of codes, i.e. complete information. No one owns *all codes*.

It should always be kept in mind that information, as a form of energy, is without time and shape. It is a higher dimension than one can think of – that is, for his brain to recognise and define. Existing knowledge of information and any attempt to define it is only an attempt to limit its capacity as information is constantly being duplicated. If a man longs to reach the realisation of teleportation, on which modern scientists are working, ask why they did not succeed. They did not because scientific knowledge so far has not clarified all this, so this process is more difficult and imperfect in practice.

Our thoughts are nothing more than 'reading' – that is, receiving, interpreting, and processing – information. Man's or the human brain is not its creator but only its interpreter, something that receives, modifies, transforms it according to man's own possibilities and needs, as I already said, and I underline it. Information retention control has always been the focus of people who belonged to 'power groups', inherent in either companies or individuals who want to save something from 'forgetting'.

In the modern Information Age, this is attempted through artificial memories or digital information carriers. But that's just a fraction of what overall information makes. All these resources are so imperfect compared to collective memory. With the advancement of technology, we create the ability to store and increase the storage capacity of information, but we can never completely save them because information is multiplied by the second. If we want to put it in a coordinate system – that is, space and time – or we define one of the formulas, it would look like this:

$$I \times Vn\ (F)$$
$$Km = T \pm 1$$

Km — collective memory
I — information
T — weather
Vn (F) — vector space

I would like to clarify this seemingly very simple formula and the expression $T \pm 1$ – because the code provides information from the 'past' and 'future'. I am talking about time inversion. For us, i.e. human civilisation, there is absolutely no sure proof of who the Creator is – the first piece of information – and since it is circulating without time and space restrictions and clear boundaries, we cannot say with certainty what will happen in the future or what really happened in the past.

Well, do we have a reliable answer to the question of how man was born to begin with? Once again, I will say that information is not created by man but by the Creator. The human brain, i.e. man, only receives, reproduces, and processes it with the help of codes.

RTS: How do you explain the loss of memory in a person?

GSF: Disorders of sight, even of memory, are related to human brain disorders. The inability to receive, recognize, or interpret information is the loss of memory or dementia, to use a generally accepted medical term. Dementia can be moderate, developed, or complete. Even in complete dementia, when a person no longer recognises the environment in which they are located nor has anything to say about it, with minimal knowledge of themselves, it is possible that there has been an inability to manage the code for receiving information because codes are, at the same time, serving us and the 'correct' way of processing information and its storage.

Theories of the onset of humankind, especially Darwin's theory, are completely absurd. They exclude everything that a person is and that he is created by the Creator as well as information or energy. Can anyone with certainty say that the human species was created? On questions of the complexity of life, even of man, science gives answers to certain time traces. If Darwin is right, why has not one man come from a monkey for a million years?

In the end, in the mid-nineteenth century, Darwin could not even know how the mechanism of evolution through natural selection could look like, i.e. he did not know anything about gene mutations, changes in viruses, bacteria, and parasites that affect changes in the human organism. He did not know anything about GMO food. He did not know much, but he claimed that man had come from the monkey. Only the Creator can establish order in many parts on the separate creation of information.

We know today that the universe is about fourteen million years old. Until a hundred years ago, we did not even know how long our planet, Earth, existed for a long time. Many details about us, about everything that surrounds us, remain quite vague, and the question of how a molecule, with the ability to reproduce and store information, was spontaneously developed from certain ingredients remains. I'm talking about DNA, which has an internal mechanism of self-esteem.

Many researchers have recently highlighted ribonucleic acid, RNA, as a possible initial form of life since RNA has the ability to transmit information, but in some cases, it can also catalyse chemical reactions in a way that DNA cannot. DNA represents in the organism something like the hard disc of a computer, a medium in which information can be stored. On the contrary, RNA is similar to storage and data storage devices. It enables the processing and transformation of data.

It is quite certain today that no serious scientist with reliability could claim that we have information about the origin of life, unless he possesses the COD to obtain this information and if it exists. But it does not mean that this will remain so in the future – that is, we will not have that information. However, we must leave something for the future, right? Most organisms that had once lived on planet Earth did not leave any trace of their existence so that every claim of a scientist is about the origin of life, even of man. One thing is certain – man has the code to recognise the 'language' of the Creator, i.e. to receive information. Without this code, life does not work.

RTS: Does the principle of receiving information work in the rest of the living world just like in a man?

GSF: Absolutely on the same principles that a human being works, so does the whole world surrounding us, which we belong to. The search for a signal that is available to the entire living world would be related to a common denominator – all organisms consist of cells, communication among cells, a collective conscientious answer to many questions, and the principle of information exchange.

Proof of such a system is free single-cell systems. There are numerous examples of animals that function by receiving information, although this has been explained by classical science as a drive, which, of course, is not true. We can, if you want, go from the amoeba. Amoeba living in the community respond to certain information received. They collect when the time is for breeding. Even half a million individuals can coordinate their activities without having even the most streamlined form of nervous system. Thus, the nervous system does not have the crucial role of 'information receiver', as classical science explains.

Also, in the case of birds, it is interesting to consider the receipt of information. Their annual migrations or shifts every autumn to the south and vice versa, from the south to the north early spring, was the subject of many studies. Bird information is not translated 'from knee to knee' in writing, which is characteristic of man, and yet they have an unmistakable 'navigation system' that leads them to their intended destination. Birds receive information on the time of movement, direction of movement, and ultimate destination from collective memory. This is mistakenly attributed to instinct. No, birds instinctively receive information from collective memory, as do many other animals, including humans.

Similar is the case with salmon. This type of fish spends a lifetime in the sea or in freshwater rivers and lakes. Salmon reside both in one and the other. They are known for crossing a long way from the ocean to their native stream. Young salmon leak out in rivers and streams. As they grow, they move downstream and ultimately get to the sea, where they grow up. A few years later, they go upstream to spill back into the rivers where they came out. There, they are streamed. I found the eggs, and eventually, they died. It's only once in your life. Salmon also use information from collective memory and infallibly find the path for long and hundreds of miles.

In addition to the above examples, it is also known that the male ostrich has a few females that strictly adhere to the order of egg laying – laying five or six eggs starting from the one at the top of the recess that he dug in the ground. The last of the eggs can be laid in time and three weeks after the first one, but all eggs are left for about six weeks later in an interval of a few hours. This fascinating endurance allows the male to take better care of the offspring, and information about the order in which the eggs are left is not based on the sounds of development that come from the eggs, as many scientists have so far explained, but on the cell communication system, as I have already said.

In addition to everything listed, there are also known 'alarm signals' transmitted by animals in certain situations. Seagulls advertise this in a specific way by warning their flock of the appearance of predators, from whose presence they receive information via communication channels. Many other animals have a specific behaviour when they receive alarm alert information, but they are not received via the senses but via communication channels that open up in specific situations in individuals. So the answer lies outside the boundaries of the normal sensory perception.

A very interesting example is bees, which function according to the unique principle of the division of labour. The jobs within one swarm are strictly determined hierarchically. From generation to generation, information is transmitted through an information field that works perfectly. In addition, the honeycomb of the perfect geometric shape that they make is confirmation that they work according to a certain 'dictation' or information on the precise way of making honey. Although the bee is an insect that has a brain that is far smaller than a human's, a large number of concepts for bees, besides the construction of the honeycomb, cannot be attributed only to motoring.

Aggressive flight: irritated bees fly to the intruder with a characteristic charge, which suggests stinging

Warning adhesion: bees stand with raised abdomen, emitting pheromones, throwing stings, wobbling wings

Antenna: mutual contact between crankshafts, without food exchange, to confirm the affiliation of the bee community

Dance tracking: bees follow the dancing of another bee to learn about the target locations of rich foods

Tracking the nuts: being part of the escort mat, occasionally licking and touching the antennae

Biting the intruder: bees sometimes do not stumble but bite

Searching for food: touching another crank's antenna to get rid of food

Short beep: a signal that bees accompany with the dance, causing discontinuation of the dance

Incubation of the litter: pressing the body of the cell with the litter for heating (by the contraction of the muscle of the thorax)

Construction of honeycomb: forming of wax-derived cells; radical, boring, and mother larvae require cells of different dimensions, which is why it is necessary for bees to possess different motor skills to be able to construct them

Buccaneer riding: in a cluster of swarms, some bees run through a cluster in a specific way to signal that the take-off moment has arrived

Matching honeycombs: closing the larva cell

Cell cleaning: removing waste from empty honeycomb cells

Chewing pollen: chewing pollen from the basket with the leg of the other crank

Whipping the hive: biting the mandible of the hive walls surrounding the honeycombs

Division community: a large number of workers, along with an old queen, leave the old hive to move to a new home; the process of preparing a divorce involves various forms of individual behaviour

Removal of corpses: removal of dead bees from a hive

Vibrating with the abdomen: the bee stands with a vibrating abdomen, often sticking to another crank during preparation for some serious activity (e.g. birth)

Egg laying: placing unprocessed eggs into the honeycomb cells

Removing the trunks: at the end of the year, the cranks bury the trunks, throw them out of the hive, and sometimes strike them

Stretching of the organs for taking food: extending the tongue to catch a small drop of nectar

Beating of wings: ventilation of the hive by wings

Nutrition of the larvae: insertion of the head into the cell to feed the larvae; vomiting of the nectar drop, which the recipient sucks

Taking food: providing the tongue between the mandibles of the other crank to accept the nectar

Accept the quality: the bee stands on its wings to spread the other bees to their mandibles (jaws)

Moving itself: cleaning itself with its lips or feet

Removing the crank: cleaning the bee from the same hive using mandibles

Watching: at the entrance of the hive, bees examine newcomers and attack potential intruders

Controlling cells with a litter: the bee inserts its head into the cell to determine the condition of the larva

Examination of potential sites for new nest: testing cavities (most commonly wood) to determine whether they are suitable for a new habitat

Side movements ('hygienic dance'): the crank is standing and swinging its body from one side to the other; this behaviour is often a consequence of being eaten by another bee

Touching the folded cells with the mouthpiece: a worker walking along a litter or a folded food reserve, touching the wax with fast movements of the mandible

Collection of nectar: sucking nectar from flowers

Nectar storage: cranks accept food from collectors, which is deposited in the medial cells

Orientation flights: flights around a hive with the goal of getting to know the characteristic environmental orientations

Packed pollen: 'solid' packing of pollen in the honeycomb cells; appears during preparation for taking the swarm to a new location

Collecting pollen: involves the collection of powdered pollen from flowers, its appearance from the bee body, and packaging into specialised hairy structures on the legs (pollen hide)

Preventing the fight between the queens: when new nuts are made, crankshafts use a variety of tactics to keep them at a distance

Resin collection: collection of resin from the trees and transporting it to the hives for pollen, where they will be used for the propolisation of the habitat

Working with resin inside a hive: sealing holes and cracks in a hive

Graveyard: falling into other hives to rob nectar

Search for food: a search for appropriate floral resources to train other bees to use them

Search for a new nest location: bees search the environment to find potential locations for the nest

Sick dance: appears at the transition between the circular and the rolling dance

'Sterzeln': elevation of the abdomen and emission of pheromones, with wings attached

Stabbing: the attack and stabbing of an animal that is 'recognised' as an intruder

Indication of a quick sweep: well-informed reconnaissance quotes a swarm according to the new location of the nest by performing striking overflows

Forming the cluster of wolves: after the division of the community, the swarm is wrapped in a temporary location – say, a branch of a tree – to search for a new habitat

Shocking dance: a special 'dance' whose signal function has not been fully clarified to date

Oscillation: stereotypical behaviour of the bee during the summer with the aim of storing a new food source or entering a hive

Unloading the pollen: the worker scratches the pollen from the leg and inserts it into the cells of the honeycomb

Dancing: a repetitive movement in the form of eight, with the aim of pointing to the location of the food source

Water collection: bees search for fresh water to suck and return to the hive

Water cooling: to prevent overheating, the bees disperse water in the honeycomb, causing its evaporation

Police control: the removal of eggs that have been laid by other cranks

Here, together with the making of honey, there are a total of sixty very complicated actions that bees organise and, according to the principle of hierarchy, practice within one swarm or community. Classical science has no answer as to how insects, like bees, can, from generation to generation, perform such complex and very precise processes, despite the fact that their brains, compared to man's, are much smaller. The only answer to this question is that bees are a classic example of establishing a communication process with the information field through certain codes.

RTS: Do plants function according to the same principle that you have already explained?

GSF: The answer is yes. The whole cosmos operates according to the same principles, and this, of course, is transmitted to the entire living world, even to inanimate matter. It has been proven that plants respond to external stimuli. So they receive information. The logical question is, can the plants communicate with one another? If we said that this can be done with amoeba – that is, single-celled organisms – by exchanging information at the cell level, why couldn't it be done with plants?

Ancient civilisations had a cult tree. The old Celts especially respected the oak and 'searched for information' through sacred rituals under its canopy. African tribes believe that ghosts, good or evil, are good and bad information in the tree. American scientist Bekster explored the possibility of perceiving the information of plants from the environment or their reaction to external stimuli. Japanese scientist Masaru Emoto did this as well. However, although experiments have confirmed that plants receive information, they have not clarified the way this process is taking place, which is exactly what I am explaining. The unique conclusion is that plants, like humans and animals, receive and exchange information. Their collective memory serves as a database of information which, 'on demand', receives certain information through the channels and codes given by the Creator.

RTS: What is important to you for the so-called opening of communication channels, i.e. getting information and processing it?

GSF: A classic example is that mothers know almost everything about the child's needs right after the birth of the child. They react before the baby wakes up, before the alarm is announced. Scientists explained this by claiming that the mother's senses immediately after delivery were much more sensitive and that, thanks to this, they responded to more subtle irritation than usual.

However, the 'maternal instinct' is not based on sharpened senses but an increased desire to receive information related to the newborn. Hence, it is logical that the mother consciously – but more often unconsciously – asks a lot of questions about her child and searches for information that enters the information field through a code that is activated by her desire to meet the needs of a newly born child who cannot tell her what she needs through articulated voice communication.

A similar situation occurs in people who have a leg or arm amputated. Dying cells also emit a signal to which living beings react. One of the most characteristic examples of this is 'phantom pain' in a man when, after arm or leg amputation, he still feels pain, tingling, itching in the area of the amputated limb. The information, as I said, is indestructible, and we receive signals such as 'phantom pain' at certain moments when the desire to continue the existence of a connection between us and the dead or dead cells continues to exist.

RTS: What is misinformation?

GSF: And misinformation is one particular kind of information. Whether it is true or not, the brain does not recognise it, but it is processed automatically, like any other piece of information. Although misinformation might be much talked about, what is essential is that it equally affects people as does information. It is complemented, multiplied in the collective consciousness. I would not be overly concerned with misinformation because something that is not in the Creator's spirit should not be favoured.

14

Orb — Information Light Particles

RTS: You mentioned experimenting with the orbs. Can you explain to us where the orbs are and what they actually represent?

GSF: Orbs are light balls. Tesla still talked about them – that is, about the light particles on which information is manifested. Each particle is scattered and has different information. The number of orbits is unlimited. They are all around us. They are the masters of the whole universe because they are particles of divine light, divine information that manifests the energy of the ether.

Orbs are information carriers, and we have them everywhere – in the air, in the water, in the land. Researching information light-emitting diodes or orbs, I dedicated years of my life to. I have renounced much for knowledge of this phenomenon, which is so far away, yet is 'at the reach of a man's hand' – that is, his understanding of himself and the world around him.

When I say that I have abandoned much of my life by exploring the orbs, I want to explain it to you a little. Namely, when 'information starts', it demands a lot of dedication – that is, attention and isolation from everything, primarily people. Any distortion of thoughts, energies, or senses from one such 'appearance' means a departure from its essence, i.e. discovering its essence. Careful study requires concentration and full focus. Any deviation from focus distorts a harmonious relationship and approach necessary for the study and complete observation of one phenomenon.

The knowledge I received by studying the orbs completely changed my previous view of the world. Orbs can be duplicated with the same information, in the same way information is continuously multiplied. Tesla claimed that he received information for his patents from the ether as well as inspiration. He also claimed that he was a constant receiver of certain information. In other words, he had adjusted his life to receiving information – loneliness, relaxation, even diet. To better collect everything from the ether. Thanks to his focus, he came up with new inventions that have had an impact on the way of life of the entirety of humanity. Even the transmission of wireless information, we have witnessed.

Orbs are, in fact, particles that represent impulse carriers or one piece or a whole series of information, regardless of whether this information relates to an individual, group, or humanity as a whole. The circles or particles form an information field in the form of a disc, a globe, a concentric aura. The human eye is a rather imperfect apparatus, as are our other senses, which we rely on every day. However, despite the limitation of the senses, we, in the search for answers to questions, open ourselves the possibility of new insights. Thus, with the help of an invention such as a digital camera, capable of recording what the human eye is not capable of, we record a phenomenon such as the orbs.

I believe that in our environment, there are animals or insects with similar abilities. Only man has not explored enough of himself and the world that surrounds him. In addition, classical science has quite limited human possibilities, also that of the rest of the living world, putting man at the forefront – that is, his performances are supreme in relation to those of the rest of the living world.

Animals, plants, and even stones correspond with the orbs. If we really want to insist on the fundamental difference between their correspondence with the orbs and what is happening in the orbs' relation, we can say that we cannot talk about spiritual reception. According to the transcendent world of animals, there is almost no relationship. It is a limiting circumstance, and it relates to exactly this tiny spark of the invention of a gift that sometimes captures a man.

In addition, only man, apparently, has the authority to receive the contents of the world of spirituality, and this is what the human spirit means – another kind of energy from what is inherent in the sense of sight or hearing, hence the specific relationship between man and the Creator, who sends him information, the driving energy – the energy of life. Information is actually a holographic collection of characters or data with all kinds of senses of multidimensional potentials. I know this sounds pretty tricky, but split this information into its components and slowly consider. You will get the answer to many questions about information.

Here is the theory of information observed from the angle of the hologram. As we have already been convinced, our senses are not perfect. Likewise, we are not aware of the perfection of certain information that our senses do not register. Because what does information do, whose reflections and orbs we are talking about? Information is the most external form of energy, constantly duplicated through space and time, and thus, data from the Creator is displayed in several forms, also in the form of the orb. So far, despite numerous attempts to explain and define information as something that exists in our world, no definition or scientific theory has fully explained the essence of information.

RTS: Are the orbs a kind of intelligence?

GSF: First, let me explain what IQ basically represents. IQ is the measure of the amount and method of processing information. A person with a higher degree of IQ, intelligence quotient, is only able to receive and process more information. Orbs are particles of consciousness and omnipresence, a reflection of the information field. So attributing an orb's measurable intelligence, like IQ, is meaningless. Emotional intelligence is something else, and we can talk about it a second time because it is quite a complex topic.

RTS: We'll stop there because we would like to explain how the orbs get information.

GSF: Namely, by the appearance of digital technology, the orbs became visible. Of course, not the naked eye but modern digital techniques record them with their 'eye'. They 'show up' on certain photos. For twenty years, we have identified the orbs with ghosts or some other thing. Today we identify them with angels, the souls of the dead, God, alien civilisation, materialised brainwaves, and so on.

Scientists also tried to define particles recorded by digital technology and came, in most cases, to the conclusion that it is dust and the reflection of dust particles, ignoring the fact that these particles are, however, significantly different from particles of ordinary dust. If previous researchers proved that all the particles were dust, that would mean that my theory is not correct. Such superficial conclusions deprived me deeply, and I entered into further research since all my observations had previously opposed their claims. I did not allow prejudices based on classical science to limit me in reflections and research.

In the end, is it not claimed from ancient times that 'everything is written down somewhere'? This is often spoken in our conversations and, in a way, indicates that the human mind has long recognised the fact that information is recorded – that is, it remains despite the flow of time. It remains permanently recorded on the 'information carriers' in the ether. These 'information carriers' are, of course, the light particles we are talking about and whose similarity to modern artificial 'information carriers' to popular CDs is more than obviously closely linked to the way of receiving and processing information.

Photo: Examples of artificial information carriers – a CD carrier, where the physical similarity with the appearance of the orb is more than obvious.

I conducted my experiments in the laboratory, in the open air, underwater, even on a plane. In the following photographs, which I am claiming to be authentic, without any processing, I will document this phenomenon.

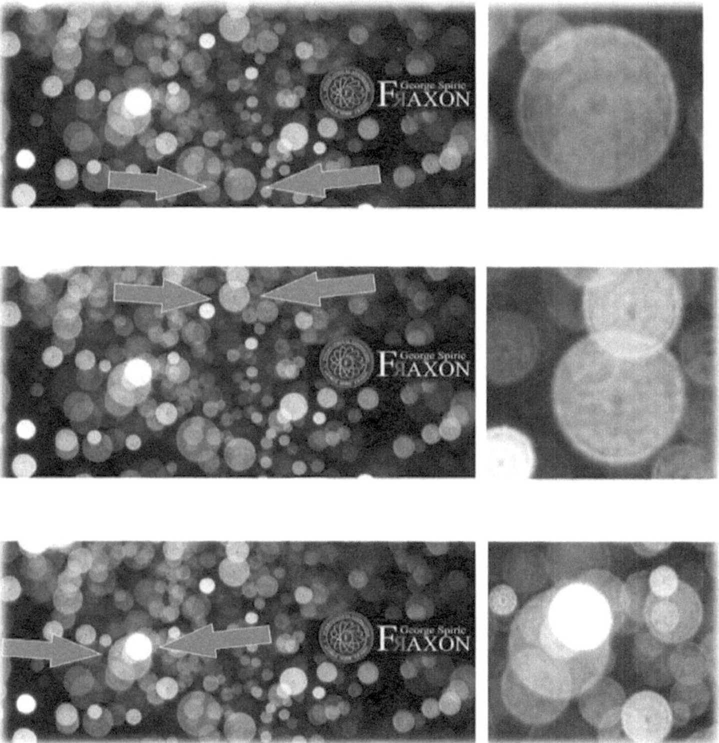

Photo: Precision separation of dust particles from other dust particles increased three times – the shape of the orb, like a CD with a clearly bound aura in the form of a light ring.

Photo: Group of orbs recorded on a plane at an altitude of over ten thousand metres.

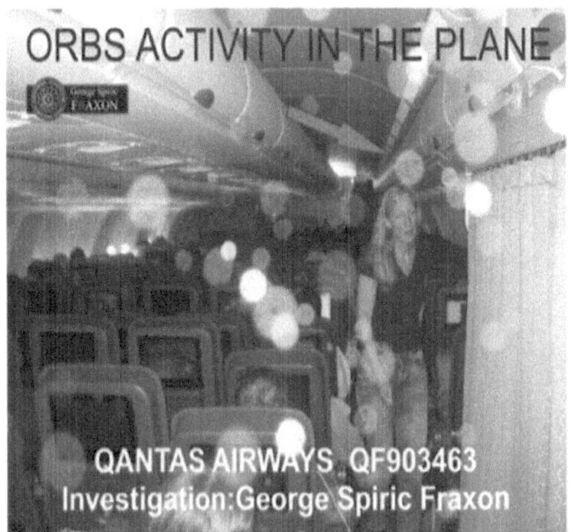

Photo: Featured and enlarged orb in the close proximity of a woman with clear outlines of the orb's intensively golden aura. The 'recorded face of a person'.

Photo: A group of orbs – 'orbs union' – on a plane shot with a digital camera at a height of ten thousand metres.

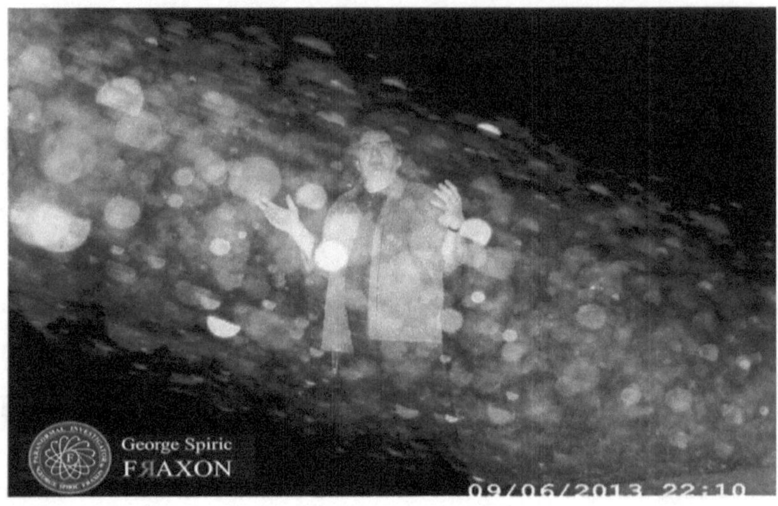

Photo: 'Orbs unions' directed, channelled.

Photo: A mirror experiment on the ground.

Photo: Measurements by nano-metres and other measuring instruments showing parameters that vary depending on the amount of information contained in the orbs.

Photo: Orbs unions photographed in Thailand in 2014, where I conducted my first orbs research underwater.

Photo: Melbourne, Australia – a photo of the clustering and compression of an orb's plasma (angel), which has a strong information field caused by a large amount of emotions.

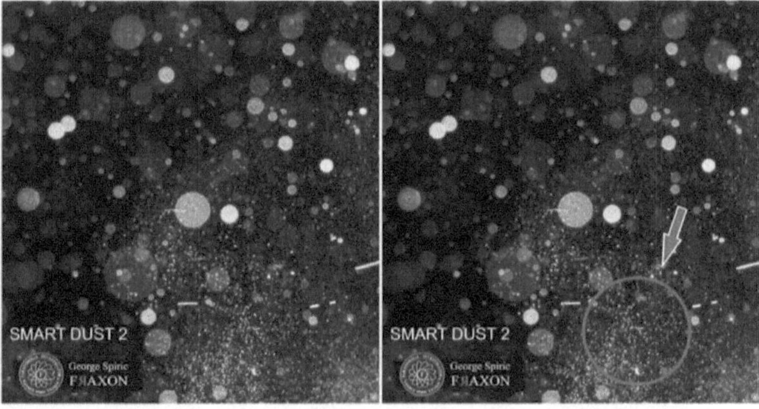

Photo: The distinction between an orb and 'smart dust' is clearly shown. Based on these comparisons, NASA made a difference and called the orbs 'smart dust'.

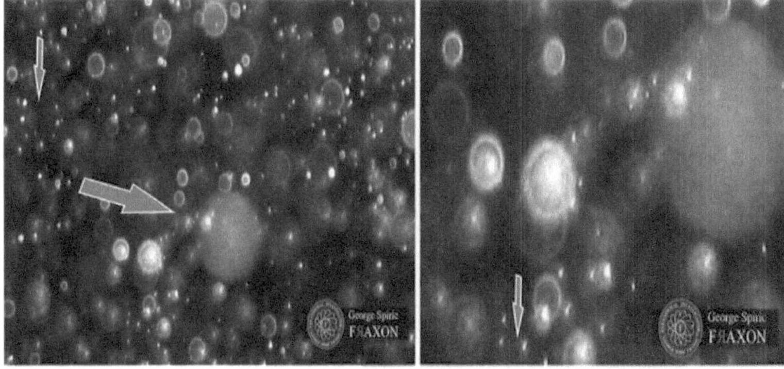

Photo: In this photograph, the particles of ordinary dust that are visibly different in physical structure from the orbs are clearly marked on this photograph. The particles of dust only reflect light. They do not have aura, the information field, and are clearly smaller than orbs.

All photos are original.

George Spiric Fraxon
3Dimensional ⇒ 4Dimensional

George Spiric
FRAXON

MELBOURNE - AUSTRALIA
George Spiric
FRAXON

MELBOURNE - AUSTRALIA
George Spiric
FRAXON

George Spiric
FRAXON
MELBOURNE - AUSTRALIA

MELBURNE - AUSTRALIA
George Spiric
FRAXON

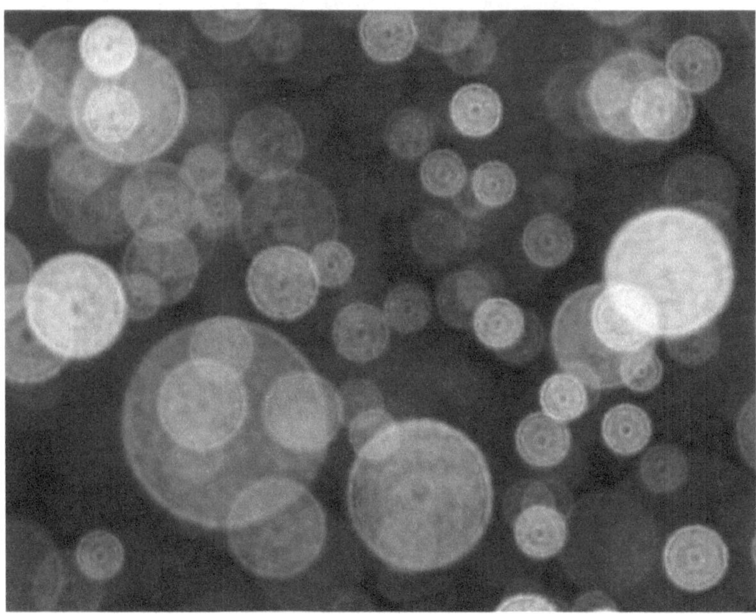

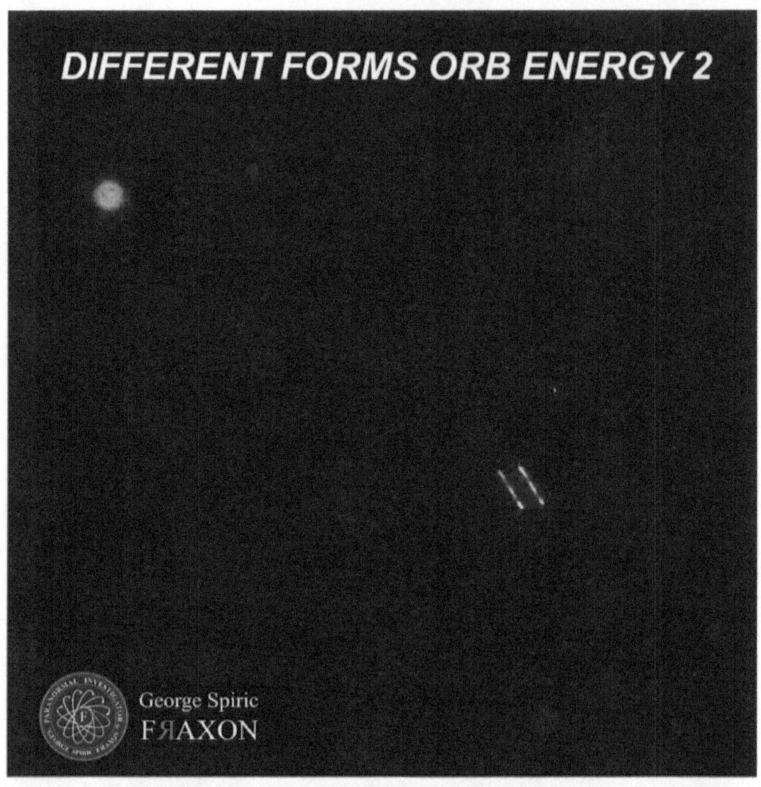

Photo: An obvious display of clearly visible variations of the orb's form.

Claims that are still stubbornly advocated by some 'researchers' are devastating cover-ups of the truth, which inevitably comes to those who strive for it. It is true that there are reflections in dust particles, but light particles, i.e. the orbs, still differ from the reflection of dust clouds. In a cubic millimetre of dust, there are over seven hundred different nano-particles of different composition.

Orbs are of a different shape and can be significantly larger. These particles 'behave' as antennae and can capture the information they fill. If you enlarge the photo in which particles of dust and orbs are recorded, a different structure is seen at first glance. The orbs generate data that they receive not only through humans but also from animals, plants, stones.

With more careful viewing and magnification of the picture, it becomes unambiguous to conclude that the dust particles have an inconsistent, 'deadened', and unregulated inner structure, while the orbs have a recognizable, clear structure with one core and an 'aura' around the last layer as a kind of shell. The difference between dust particles and orbs is that the orbs carry information. I proved this in my experiments, and I am writing a book on all my research on this topic, which I hope will clarify many things that have remained beyond the reach of human knowledge.

Based on the research I have been conducting for more than a decade around the world and using special measuring instruments, I recorded the movement of orbs, their grouping, appearance, disappearance — their essence. Separating dust particles is a routine matter, and they are completely easy to separate if you know the characteristics of information light particles, which have a specific aura, the halo that is bound by each orb.

RTS: How can all the orbs manifest themselves?

GSF: Very often they happen to be grouped, but that's not the rule. Their size, number, and colour depend on many factors, and basically everything is the type or origin of information they carry. In many of them, there are more or less clear contours and images, even human characters. In different places, they surround us at any time. Wherever I travel, I study their appearance, from shapes to frequencies.

There are people around the globe who are sending photos that have recorded this phenomenon. So this phenomenon is characteristic of either the end of the planet, not only certain areas, or of those who are 'given' to see them, i.e. communicate with them. Interest in orbs is extremely high in the world, but manipulations regarding their appearance are very common. Wherever I travelled, I personally investigated whether their phenomenon manifests itself in different places and came to a great experience – the orbs are omnipresent informative light particles.

Thanks to my tireless research spirit that is constantly searching for answers to many questions, we now have a clear answer to whether the orbs exist and what they represent. But I will describe all this in detail in my next book and provide humanity with answers not only to this but also to many other questions because I was exploring the orbs, with amazing observations that were at hand but hidden from people.

RTS: Now we are completely changing the attitude towards this phenomenon because we have come across completely different interpretations of the orbs that were contradictory, brought a lot of confusion, and were rather vague. How do you comment on this?

GSF: I will try to be as clear as possible. I might have been reluctant to comment on the 'reach' of other 'experts' before, but after so many years of research and results, I simply have the right to tell the truth or my beliefs about it. It is well known that religious people consciously and unconsciously seek confirmation of the existence of what they believe. For example, Christians believe in Christ, and very often it happens that in nature, they receive forms that resemble a person's likeness. The misuse of a human being and their faith is common among those who would benefit from their desire to find confirmation of the existence of what they believe.

Only a few of them suspected that it was oversized information that simply destroyed the device's memory, but that was not enough. I wanted to know unambiguously what was going on. Of course, after a long period of research, today I can certainly claim that the orbs carry certain information of a smaller or larger capacity, and it is not always compatible with the memory of devices that this phenomenon wants to record.

RTS: You claim that the orbs are information carriers?

GSF: Orbs are particles that are themselves in the form of a disc, a physical carrier – artificial memory. As we know, the devices we use to record and store information have limited memory. I tried to do a series of experiments with a camera with a larger memory card. Everything was fine until the moment I tried to transfer it to a computer that had less memory than what took up space on the camera's memory. The computer simply 'burst'. After the expertise of IT experts who were also involved in IT forensics, I came to the conclusion that everything from the computer memory was simply deleted. It has become more than clear that one or a group of orbs can carry with them a large amount of information that occupy a large memory space – that is, they exceed the capacity of the artificial memory of the devices we use.

Orbs take up to ten to a hundred times more memory when they zoom in or zoom out. The devices with which I worked with a group of assistants discovered that orbs spend more battery life than in ordinary work. Very often they would be blocked when recording an orb's manifestation. The orbs may appear individually or in a group. Many people call this phenomenon a 'guppy orb', 'entity', and the like. The appearance itself, the orb's form, is quite different, and unlike dust particles, orbs have a kind of aura.

The occurrence of the grouping of information light particles is called an orbs union. This is a phenomenon when we have the appearance of several orbs in one small space that can be interconnected and separated, of different sizes, colours, and intensities. Each of them carries out certain information or a set of information. Separating the orb from dust results in a specific phenomenon. Namely, the information light particles in the orbs union form a plasma that initiates various phenomena, such as the reflection of the internal state of the one who sees or invokes them.

Even with a subconscious tendency to materialise our thoughts, this information is recorded in the orb or series of particles that form a certain shape or light reflection in the form of orbs. It is an energy record, the information that the 'X' particles form in the ether. This information remains forever in the ether. On artificial memories, CD-ROMs, microchips, sound recordings, and pictures can be made. On orbs, besides sound or image, an energy record is recorded for information related to our emotional, spiritual state.

I believe that with this, we have opened up a whole new field of human knowledge and search for many answers to questions, but I will document my many years of research related to the orbs in a documentary in my next book. I would not want the knowledge I had come to kept jealously for myself or for fear of keeping away from the public the truth I had come to in investigating information light particles. I'll share it with those who are searching for the truth in my next book because the truth is the holy grail from which the brank only drink.

Search for Answers: Experience of the Editor of *The Energy of Life*

[Dali's bench]

'Time does not exist. There are only watches.'

I will start with the picture of Dali's benches, whose form reminds me of the fact that 'time does not exist, only watches', as claimed by a great controversial artist who left a huge stamp on twentieth-century artistic creation. Instead of talking, I decided to share with my readers my unprecedented experience that happened in the middle of the creation of *The Energy of Life*, and I call it the 'search for answers'. I will try to authentically explain to you what I have experienced, for which I did not have an answer and which was more than obvious between the lines of *The Energy of Life*.

With my wife, I decided that for our short break, we would spend our holidays in Egypt after a long consideration of whether it was a very convenient moment because both of us have numerous business obligations in Belgrade. I note that the latest preparations for the publication of *The Energy of Life* were already underway. Regardless of everything, we decided, 'When if not now?' That summer had its charms, which we began to feel only after two days, when we managed to somehow 'shuffle' from everyday life, work, obligations, and everything that we had left in Belgrade. For exactly two years, we worked without respite, without rest, on every business.

Completely unexpectedly, something happened to me, during which, at first, I could not 'come to myself' from a huge number of questions that were imposed, checked, self-proclaimed. Namely, I woke up at precisely 5:27 a.m. Now that I look at it, it's true. The time was shown in red numbers on a digital clock that was standing on a nightstand near my head. The curtains on the large glass door were spaced so that it appeared to me like a 'cloudy morning'. I thought that it would cheer me up and of how I had forgot to drink a drug that, otherwise, I would drink in the evening before bedtime. I went to the bathroom to take it as necessary. The film is exactly marked by the day of the week for each tablet for one month. I did not drink the one for Thursday. Otherwise, I drank another type of medicine every morning, hormonal, necessary for the functioning of the thyroid gland. I thought at that moment that the distance between the two treatments and tablets would be small. From the bathroom, I went to the table with a bottle of water to drink 'Thursday'. I returned the bottle on the table and lay back in bed.

I was awakened again by the need to urinate. I got up from the bed and looked again, I do not know why, in the direction of the clock. It was 2:10 a.m. Soon after that moment, the digital timer showed 2:11 a.m. At first, I thought that I had woken up subconsciously to drink the medicine that I had forgot to take that evening. But something was, however, unusual to me. I was almost sure that I had taken it. I went to the bathroom and took the medicine box from the drawer. I saw that I had taken the tablet marked on the foil as 'Thursday'. There was darkness outside. I went out on the terrace. The hotel complex was glittering from night lamps. In the distance, a continuous chain of highway lights was illuminated.

A strange feeling overtook me, and countless information simply rushed through me. Re-examining what had happened turned into questions, and I abandoned the search for answers to the questions, asking what had dominated. There were some sort of 'external–internal' information rows, among which lay the terms *weather*, *disharmony*, *particle dualism*, and *inaccuracy of pi*. It does not amount to 3.14 but 3.17. And not only that. In front of my eyes was a formula. Persistent by nature, I asked what it could be. Later on, after returning to Belgrade, I wrote it just the way it was 'shown' then. To my surprise, it's no longer so much except that it's incredibly engraved in my memory. By searching the internet, I came to the first equation that connects the wavelength with the particle pulse.

I will return to this 'night' or 'morning'. In those moments, I had the dominant feeling as if I had the answers to 'all' questions, as if my knowledge was gathered in my hands when there was human civilisation – except for the answer to the question on 'weather disharmonies' – a feeling that cannot be described as easily but is the closest thing to the word. I was lying down and trying to conceal my thoughts and fear that had come out. Something told me that I was not looking at anything more in the room. Not looking back in the direction where my wife was sleeping, I fell asleep again.

What really shocked me was that I had woken up at 6:10 a.m. I was shaken. The first thing I did when I opened my eyes was to look at the timer and then through the glass door. It was morning. I got up from the bed, went back to the bathroom. I looked at the medicine box, in whose foil was missing 'Thursday'. So I drew on, for the second time, on Friday, 1 September 2017, I guess? Asking what was going on, I drank my morning drugs and prepared Nescafé. I went out to the terrace and searched the coffee for the answer to just one question – how is it possible to wake up at 5:27 a.m. and then at 2:10 a.m. and again at 6:10 a.m. on the 'same day'?

I was reviewing everything that had happened, 're-watching the movie' in my head. These are moments when you examine your mental health, memory, subconscious mind, consciousness, existence. I had the need to tell my wife everything, and at the same time, I was tormented by her probable reaction because I could not explain to myself everything that had happened to me, especially the 'external' information flow. Although we have great trust in each other and share experiences that can be attributed to everything but a 'daily coincidence', I was a bit embarrassed because I could not figure out what was happening on my own.

She joined me on the terrace. Only after drinking coffee, I told her what had happened and wondered if she had an answer, any kind. She told me that this was my experience, that she was convinced that it was not by chance that I had experienced it, and that the answer surely awaited me somewhere. She told me to record everything, not to forget something in time.

Fast as a cannon, I replied, 'Such a thing cannot be forgotten. I remember every detail, and I know that I will stay here, without any deleted information, no matter how hard I try not to think about it.'

The 'case' was so wanted that the next morning, we both woke up at five fifteen. The outside was shining, or it was a 'cloudy morning'. This is the part of the morning when the sun does not completely 'come off' from the horizon. Well, now you understand what I told you about when it was cloudy when I had woken up at 5:27 a.m. Also, on the 'case' of waking up that night at about two o'clock in the morning, I aroused my wife and described everything in detail to her while I was 'checking' myself, what had happened to me, and how it was possible. In the distance glittered a series of luminaries along the highway, inside a hotel complex that was 'like on the palm'. From our terrace glittered night lamps along the path between the villa. All the details that I had told her, she had the opportunity to see within a couple of hours – if it was the right timing.

Looking for answers to ongoing questions upon returning to Belgrade, I also found that the approximation of ϖ as $(16/9)^2 = 3.160493$ was recorded in the Egyptian Rhind Mathematical Papyrus, dated from the twentieth century BC. So this is one of the answers, not very clear because I still cannot connect anything except that 3.16 is correct, not 3.14. The other answers, I suppose, will come to as well as to what had happened to me. I was thinking about Kozier's claim that 'time is a fundamental and general cosmic force', but this did not encourage answers to the puzzle of what had happened to me.

My conversation with George about this was inevitable. Of course, I told him all in one breath. He asked me to slowly tell him about every part of that 'event'. He returned me several times, asked me to concentrate on the details and returned again, and asked me to talk slowly, ask countless questions, and concluded that I had a real experience and that each one would be 'easier for me, more acceptable, and would bring new information to him'. I was wondering if he was sure that this would repeat again.

He replied with a smile, 'Once you learn to swim, it does not pose a problem to you later.' And after a break, he added, 'Well, you know what kind of book you're doing.'

It has already happened that we are discussing many details during the creation of *The Energy of Life* and that our opinions match, or we have the feeling that we have already 'shared information' about it before. Does a channel open? Do we get a code for all of us who get into these turbulent lines of self-knowledge that George shares with us unselfishly? I'm still looking for an answer, and he seems to be there. Maybe he is already among us.

Guided by the fact that this work was created as a product of the answer to the questions of the scientific team that led the conversation with George Špirić Fraxon, we considered that the best review is exactly the word of the readers. That is, the best and the most disagreeable opinions about the book will be given by those who will present their independent critical judgements on this, the truly unusual and unselfishly shared experience and knowledge the author has come to experience during his decades-long practice and research.

When it was announced that this work would soon be published through social networks and other means of communication, there began to appear many who were interested in how to come to have this book. He had authored a few that were controversial and showed the greatest interest in sending a transcript of his conversation with the science team and asked them to read it as soon as possible by insisting, only at one time, to sincerely give opinions and criticism and to ask questions about possible uncertainties.

We are convinced that the previous readers have very sincerely shared their personal impressions of everything they have learned, felt, or experienced reading this book, revealing themselves and the world around them. Considering that each of you can and should experience this book in your own way, on the following pages, we give you an insight into just a few of the opinions that the first readers have said about this book, from which, at first glance, comes the unique view that this book opens up a new horizon in thinking and on life and represents a 'window into our reality'.

Review of George Špirić Fraxon's *The Energy of Life*

The book connects the spiritual and physical aspects of life. Once you have read the book, there is a magnetic force that pushes you to want to read it again. The feeling is phenomenal as this book opens doors for everything that is unknown. The key findings are the light particles that are the 'energy of life', that provides us with the life itself.

After reading this book, I have adopted the opinion that from one moment to another, I was discovering a new world on subjects such as telepathy and intuition. Tesla works well in a quiet way with what I found reading *The Energy of Life* as there is an existing parallel in relation to the work of the future, where the laws of nature prevail and reveal a great deal. I would like to take the pleasure to thank you for all the answers this book has given me as this book clearly channels in the opening the key question to life – who am I?

George Fraxon challenges us to live in the present moment and thereby transform our consciousness and live in the joy of being. George's book offers a step-by-step approach to a life of balance, courage, abundance, and joy. It's just a great book. If you want to improve your life, look no further than this book. You can implement the simple things from this book into your daily life to find the happiness you are looking for.

The Energy of Life was definitely an eye-opener on so many levels. I thoroughly enjoyed reading this book as it contains real facts of reading certain concepts and principles so that I could better understand his material life, which is necessary for understanding life on a holistic level. It's brilliantly written in a question-and-answer format which touches on various aspects of life as a whole.

Once again, I thank the writer for sharing this gem and equipping us with the necessary knowledge and tools.

— LS (Melbourne, Australia)

Dear George,

I am quite sure that it was not easy for you to succeed in translating your great experience from long-lasting hypnotherapeutic and scientific work into such a clear and direct way on paper. You are obviously the man by the cosmic but not earthly principles who understands that the essence of our lives is in the material world, in the acquisition and transfer of knowledge.

The words of this book and the wired thoughts that accompany them are offered to the reader as a sincere, friendly gift about whose usability he himself decides. Your conversations have no calculations. You are honest and offer your insights and experiences openly and unbaffled. That's why it's easy to understand and brotherly accept and respect.

Your book answers and asks questions. You open new facets and paint new colours with familiar ones. By doing this, you are given the opportunity to express, inspire, liberate, and mobilise all those who have a reality-television reality, are poor, and feel that 'there is something there'.

For all that, I sincerely congratulate you on the work you give us, on the thoughts that are sent to us.

Stay in health. Let the Lord continue to give you such creative and research energy and continue to rejoice in your new books, innovative ideas, and unique scientific creations.

All the best,
OZ

The author thanks all those who have so far made their impressions of the book and invites you to continue submitting your comments, questions, and impressions, offering information that you will receive in the meantime.

Foreign Words and Expressions

Acupuncture
Treatment of pain relief and certain diseases with the help of thin needles that stab the patient at precisely defined points. It developed in China about five thousand years ago. The word *acupuncture* comes from the Latin words *acus* (needle) and *pungera* (stings).

Adrenaline
One of the stress hormones. Because of the stress reaction, adrenaline secretion from the adrenal gland occurs. The blood flows to almost all organs, causing the following changes: increased heart rate and strength, narrowing of blood vessels of the peripheral tissue, and the expansion of the blood vessels of the heart, the brain, some muscles and other important organs, and the bronchi.

Aesthetics
Science of sensory observation. In a narrow sense the science of the beautiful, especially about art as the fullest expression of what is beautiful. The science of meaning for art and artistic taste.

Amoeba

One-celled animal belonging to the root group. It lives in sludge and on the leaves of aquatic plants. It is 0.01–0.5 mm long. The shape of the body of the amoeba changes as it starts, with the edges that we call false legs or pseudopods.

Amnesia

Loss of memory for a certain period or certain events. It most commonly occurs as a result of brain trauma or pathological changes in some brain areas but can also occur as a result of the excessive intake of psychoactive agents or an intense adverse experience (e.g. stress). It can be temporary or permanent. The organic causes of amnesia usually lead to the forgetfulness of everything that happened in a certain period, while psychogenic amnesia leads to the inability to recall only some events.

Anaesthetic

Substance intended for anaesthesia, i.e. the state of an organism characterised by a loss of memory, loss of pain, loss of muscle tone, loss of reflex movements, and loss of consciousness.

Anamnesis

Discussion with the patient to collect all information which is essential for discovering the actual nature of the disease and correct diagnosis. The length of the interview depends on the expertise of the examiner and the nature of the disease. During the interview, the examiner must distinguish important from insignificant data, and the questions asked and the data collected must not disturb the authority of the patient. Therefore, for a quality history, it is necessary for the examiner to build a backbone in the patient, thereby avoiding the release of significant data on the current disease. Anamnesis is the basis and most important part of the procedure for diagnosing the disease, and many diseases can be diagnosed after a well-taken history.

Anthropologist

A scientist who studies human life and culture, similarities and differences among people, how people live, what they do, what they think, and how they relate to the environment. In addition, the anthropologist also studies how the human race evolved and how human societies emerged and disappeared.

Artefact

Every object that a person uses which he has made or corrected. Artefacts can be both finished products and residues in the technological process.

Asthma

Constricting of the airways, often chronic, characterised by different and recurring symptoms. Common symptoms include severe breathing, coughing, tightness in the chest, and shortness of breath.

Aura

In esoteric, occult learning and parapsychology, only individual people can see the fluid light surrounding the human figure. Aura is something like an 'energy envelope' that not only covers and protects the human soul but also allows it to communicate with the universe of living and non-living things. In psychiatry are relatively short and intense subjective experiences that precede and suggest epileptic seizures. Visual, auditory, or olfactory hallucinations can occur in these short-term ecstatic states.

Cardiopulmonary Resuscitation (CPR)

The combination of median measures of revitalisation that are undertaken to restore normal life functions to a patient who has experienced a respiratory failure and/or heart failure.

Cerebral Cortex

The outer layer of the brain's nervous tissue in humans and other mammals.

Chemotherapy

Systemic treatment and control or malignant diseases (tumours) with chemical substances of natural or synthetic origin, also called antitumor drugs, cytotoxic drugs, or cytostatics. For this type of therapy, the name chemotherapy is accepted because with this method of treatment, the growth of malignant cells and tumour tissue is controlled by a chemical route.

Chi

According to Chinese traditional belief, the life-giving white light that flows through the human and connects it with the universal life force. The Japanese call it *ki* and the Indian Ayurveda *prana*.

Clinical Death

Heart failure (Latin *institio cordis*) is an abrupt stop of normal blood circulation because of the inability of the heart to properly counter-balance. It represents an urgent condition in which a certain percentage of patients can be restored to normal if medical intervention is rapid.

Code/Coding

The process of converting data to the required format. In computer technology, it is translated as a series of characters (letters, numbers, symbols) in a specialised digital format used for transmission or storage.

Coherent

Connected, held together. The concept that signifies that there are several different ideas, thoughts, subjects, and objects combined in the whole.

Concept

The desire to maintain a certain position. The meaning of words in a particular context. The abstraction of reality in our thoughts as well as its symbolic representation. Words that are synonymous are the same concepts. When we say that two sentences are synonymous with each other, then we can say that their purpose is to maintain the position of the same intent. The concept is often analysed in the context of complex forms or schedules or even ways of thinking and action and may have the result of different meanings.

Confusion

Mixing different things, clutter, non-discrimination.

Consensus

It represents the agreement or the identity of the opinion of two or more persons on a question.

Continuum

Extensible size, continuous size, whole before parts.

Defibrillation

Application of controlled electric shock for the purpose of establishing a normal rhythm of the heart. It is performed using special medical devices, defibrillators, whose electrodes are placed on the chest or, if it is open, directly to the heart.

Dominant

The one who rules, the master – superior, major, predominant.

Dysfunctional

Poor work or interruption in the work of a body organ or function. The term *dysfunction* is characterised by a disorder in a function that is caused by the effects of a social phenomenon or group or individual activity. Also, this term is also used in terms of discrepancies in the functioning of an organism as a whole, a certain organ, or some physiological, psychological, or social function.

Electroencephalograph

A device that records and graphically displays electrical currents in the brain. The resulting diagram is known as the electroencephalogram

(EEG), earlier through special feather-sensitive sensors plotted on paper
and now more often represented as a digital drawing using a computer.

Emotion

Emotions are specific relationships of a person towards oneself, specific
objects or phenomena, and other people. Emotions emerge when
something is important to us. The occurrence of emotions cannot be
caused by someone else. Emotions affirm or threaten.

Emotional Intelligence

It marks the ability to create skills and competences that give the
person the ability to rationally handle the demands and pressures of the
environment. In a wider sense, it represents a set of multiple abilities –
self-comprehension, self-control, self-confidence, and empathy. It is not
the opposite but only a different complementary ability in relation to
rational intelligence.

Engram

Permanent change of an organic substance that comes as a result of the
influence of irritation, sensory impressions, etc. The term *engram* was
first used by German biologist Richard Semon in his book *The Mneme*
in 1904. He marked the neural phenomenon of unique memory with
him. The engram is one of the constant changes in the nervous system
that conserves the experiential facts in time. The term was later taken
over by neurology to hypothetically denote the traces of memory that
were preserved or as a postulate of physical or bio-chemical changes in
the nerve tissue representing memory.

Entropy

The tendency of the natural system to spontaneously transition into
a state of greater disorder, a measure of system disorder. The greatest
systemicity of the system is at a temperature equal to absolute zero.

Epilepsy

A group of long-standing neurological disorders characterised by seizures. These seizures are episodes that can vary from shorter and almost imperceptible to long periods of strong twitching. In epilepsy, seizures are usually repeated and do not have an immediate underlying cause. Attacks that occur because of a specific cause are not considered epilepsy.

Epinephrine Injection

A special type of injection that is given to a patient whose heart has stopped working.

Esoteric

It denotes a set of learning and knowledge that deals with the study of the law of visible and invisible worlds. The term also signifies a secret form of religious learning. It also signifies the totality of esoteric knowledge and practices understood as a unified whole.

Esperanto

A planned language created for an international second language. Its basic characteristics were compiled by Ludwig Lazarus Zamenhof in 1887. Today Esperanto is used in various spheres of life, including travel, correspondence, cultural exchange, and literature. In some schools, it is taught optionally to this day.

Ether

The word is derived from the Greek word αιθηρ, which means 'sluggish, burning'. It relates to a space far above the clouds. In alchemy and philosophy, it is the fifth element – besides water, earth, fire, and air – in which all the elements of the cosmos extend.

Преведи

Ethics

A philosophy that includes the systematisation, defence, and recommendation of the concepts of right and wrong behaviour. The term *ethics* is derived from the ancient Greek words ἠθικός (*ethikos*) and ἦθος (*ethos*) with the meaning of habits or customs. Ethics, along with aesthetics, falls into a common field of philosophy called axiology or value theory. It deals with the study of morality and the notions of good and right. Each ethical theory contains at least two components or theories: one that determines what is good or worthy and one that determines what is right.

Euphoria

Feeling pleasant. A state in which a person feels unusually comfortable, is content with himself. Thoughts and feelings that are full of tranquillity and serenity. This kind of feeling also occurs in various mental and nervous diseases and then in tuberculous patients, drug addicts, and alcoholics.

Explanation

Comes from the Latin word *explicare* – to explain, interpret, clarify. It is used to indicate all details with all the necessary data.

Fascinating

One who behaves or works in a special, enchanting, original way.

Frequency

Form of periodic change of some size, number of full oscillations (flickering, flicker, cycles) in unit time. The measuring unit for frequency in the International System of Units (SI) is hertz, one oscillation per second, marked by Hz.

Frigidity

A set of different disorders of normal sexual drive. This term is obsolete from a professional point of view but continues to be used in everyday speech. In medical terminology, the following terms are used: *hypoactive sexual instinct, inhibited sexual drive, sexual aversion, reduced libido, anaphrodisiac*, etc. It is used in the sense of an emotional/sexual 'cold' or sexual disorder consisting of reduced ability for sexual excitement or an orgasmic experience, primarily in women. In principle, a man can have the same symptoms. Although this disorder can occur because of physical illness, such as a hormonal disorder, this is usually not the case. According to modern concepts, this term is multidimensional because of psychodynamic reasons, and a deep psychological treatment is required. The most common causes are depression, fears, and post-traumatic stress (say, after a violent sexual relationship), or it can be an adverse effect of some drugs, especially opiates. Frigidity can be manifested in various forms: reduced sexual desire (libido), sexual irritation disorders, or orgasm disorders, all of which fall into sexual dysfunction. Sexual activity can, in some cases, be painful. Some patients have never experienced a pleasant physical experience, even through masturbation.

Gene

A physical and functional inheritance unit that transmits a hereditary message from generation to generation, making it an integral part of the DNA needed for the synthesis of one protein or one RNA molecule. Genes are strung along chromosomes. A gene for a particular property is always in the same place on a chromosome called a gene locus.

Genetics

Scientific discipline of biology on inheritance and variation in living organisms. Provides new ways to study the function of the gene, such as the analysis of genetic interactions. In the body itself, genetic information is found in chromosomes, which are presented to chemical structures such as DNA molecules.

Genetic Mutations

Changes in the sequence of nucleotides in DNA that are permanently retained and transferred to the next generation of cells. The variability of the individuals in the population most contribute to the mutation. These are sudden hereditary changes that can affect parts of or whole chromosomes (chromosomal aberrations or changes in the number or chromosome build-up).

Guru
Teacher or leader of some idea. Religious title for a spiritual teacher in Hinduism, Sikhism, and Tantric Buddhism. In the modern Western use of the word *guru*, this can signify a person who attracts and brings together supporters with his or her religious or philosophical teaching.

Harmonisation
Adjustment of the existing with the necessary conditions.

Hindu Veda
Sanskrit *véda*/वेद, meaning knowledge. The name for the extensive corpus of texts that originated in ancient India. They are considered the earliest form of literature in the Sanskrit and oldest scriptures of Hinduism.

Hippocampus
Brain structure located in the underlying part, under the bark of the big brain, and which has a horseshoe shape. This structure is part of the limbic system and plays an important role in the regulation of emotions and behaviours but is considered to play a more important role in memory processes and spatial navigation.

Homeopathy
The course in alternative medicine founded in 1796 by Samuel Hahnemann (1755–1843) based on his doctrine to 'treat similarly', in which the substance that causes certain symptoms of illness in healthy people cures similar symptoms in patients.

Hypnosis
Method for bridging the conscious and the subconscious mind, with the establishment of acceptable selective thinking.

Hypnotherapy

A set of hypnotic techniques that are applied for therapeutic purposes for solving psychic, emotional, physiological, and behavioural problems.

Hypnotic Regression

A therapeutic method that allows access to distant memories stored in the file of our soul. In this way, we can see in our minds the whole flow of previous lives and evolutionary development.

Hysteria

Nervous disease characterised by certain mismatches of character, increased irritability and sensitivity of the senses, insufficiency of self-control, susceptibility to external influences, and vibrant imagination. For example, a patient has a feeling that some ball is climbing on his eyebrow. He has nerve pain, a headache at one point of the skull, cramping attacks (laughter, wages, etc.), severe joint pain, insensitivity (usually in one half of the soul), etc.

Inhibition

Keeping some organic action or function, willingness, or involuntary physiological action. Psychological prevention by volition or instinctual and subconscious.

Intimate

Inside, personal, cordial, friendly, e.g. intimate friendship, close relationship.

Implication

Complication, involvement in a process or an event.

Irritation

Anger.

IQ (Intelligence Quotient)
A numerical indicator of the degree of intelligence development. The determination of IQ is performed using intelligent tests adapted for a certain age and population and belongs to the domain of psychologists. The test result or IQ is obtained by dividing the mental age by the test results or calendar age (in months).

Loyalty
It denotes an internal connection and the expression of that connection through behaviour towards a person, group, or community. Loyalty means that the value system is shared with the rest of the community and that the views of the community are defended even when there is a different opinion. Loyalty is always voluntary and is shown in the behaviour towards those with whom it feels connected as well as towards third parties.

Manipulation
The use of different data or information for the purpose of 'seduction of the public' – that is, directing attention to that message or the meaning that the author wishes, regardless of the validity of the data, to be challenging. It is used in all spheres of life and in social work often means displaying the state of an individual or family that indirectly needs to support an intention or goal that does not otherwise arise from legal or other local regulations. Often, in psychology, it is also used in the meaning of a special manipulative versus verbal ability.

Medicine
Used for healing.

Meditation
The calm state of the organism. Relaxing the mind or 'not thinking'. In religion, spiritual discipline and concentration on the inner mental states, on the challenge of vision, enlightenment, and the mystical experience of merging with God or the world beyond.

Memory

The process of conscious beings in which the nervous system permanently or temporarily stores certain data. The memory can be such that it can be reproduced later or again or such that data cannot be reproduced but only recognised in re-encounters. In a wider sense, memory can refer to the storage of data in biological and technical systems (e.g. computer memory).

Mesmerism

Learning and treatment of magnetism by Franz Mesmer (1734–1815), the founder of the study of animal magnetism.

Messiah

The bearer and preacher of saving ideas. The saviour.

Metadata

Data describing the characteristics of a source in digital form. The 'data' of data. It is useful when viewing, downloading, and documenting some content. In digital terms, these are 'structured data that describe, explain, locate, or, in some other way, make it easier to manage resources'.

Migraine

A chronic disease with a very pronounced pulse-like headache that is often associated with a range of symptoms by the autonomic nervous system. It lasts from two to seventy-two hours. Other symptoms may include nausea, vomiting, photophobia (sensitivity to light), phonophobia (sound sensitivity), and pain that usually increases with physical activity. About a third of patients with migraines experience aura symptoms: transient disturbances of vision, feeling, speech, or motor skills that indicate the sudden onset of a headache.

Minor

Less valuable, insignificant, negligible.

Modify

To limit or restrict. To measure how to do it. To realise it on the right scale. To shape it.

Motive/Motivation

Concepts from psychology that represent factors that encourage the movement of the activity of the individual, cause certain behaviour, maintain it, and direct it towards a goal.

Mystification

Deception, confusion.

Myths

Fairy tales about events from the lives of supernatural and divine beings in which these divine beings descend to Earth and live and work as people and with whom they often associate and perform many weird and heroic ventures. We have the most beautiful examples of bribery in classical myths, especially Greek mythology.

Nano-particles

Particle size between one and one hundred nano-metres. In modern science, it is explained as a small object that behaves as a whole in relation to movement and properties.

Nucleotide Sequence (Nucleic Acid)

The sequence or primary structure of nucleic acid is a composition of atoms constituting nucleic acid and chemical bonds that connect these atoms. Nucleic acids, such as DNA and RNA, are unbranched polymers, and this specification is equivalent to indicating the nucleotide sequence constituting the molecule. The sequence is written as a string of letters that denote real or hypothetical nucleic acids.

Observation

Collection of data on phenomena through immediate sensory observation.

Palpation

Regarding the mode of diagnosis, palpatorial examination means a medical examination of the painful position with a gentle touch of the hand.

Paranoia

Disturbance of the mind. A kind of madness.

Phenomenon

Every occurrence in the spiritual and the external world, which is shown to our perception (senses). It is extremely difficult to explain rare phenomena.

Pheromones

Chemical messages transmitted outside the body, and the result is a direct developmental impact on changes in the behaviour of the recipient. There are alarm pheromones, trace pheromones, sexual pheromones, and many others.

Phobias

A particular form of fear that is bound to specific objects, situations, places, or activities. People who experience phobic fear are aware that it is unrealistic, illogical, or even excessive. The word *phobia* comes from the Greek word *phobos*, which means 'escape, horror, panic, fear'.

Photosynthesis

The process of converting light energy into chemical energy and its storage in the form of sugar molecules. The photosynthesis process takes place in plants as well as in some bacteria and algae which have chlorophyll in their cells.

Physiology

A science that deals with the study and interpretation of physical and chemical factors responsible for the emergence, development, and flow of life, with a particular emphasis on mechanisms that control and regulate life processes. It also deals with the way in which all living beings function, from the simplest viruses to complex multicellular organisms such as man.

Pigment

Coloured matter in animal and plant cellular tissues, found in particular pigment cells (chromatophores). Coloured matter, paint, make-up.

Post-hypnotic Suggestion

The method by which a hypnotist, during a hypnotic session, can suggest something that a person will remember when the hypnotic state passes.

Potential

Power, force, strength, ability that a thing contains in itself. Reviving force, life force, driving force.

Practice

Exercise, performance of work, experience (e.g. all traders' clients, all patients of one doctor).

Practitioner

One who does work. Skilled and experienced in a business. A man who easily and skilfully finds himself in business.

Preliminary

Introductory. It represents an expression for something that is initial, but it is assumed that it can be changed over time.

Profit

Indicates net profit, i.e. earnings, positive differences in the proportions invested and obtained. It also indicates a positive investment income by an individual or a business operation.

Psyche
Soul, spirit. The principle of life. The basis of life.

Psychosomatic Disorder
Organic, physical disorder of psychogenic origin. This includes any
disease caused by long-lasting stress or the chronic influence of negative
emotions: stomach ulcer and duodenal ulcer, digestive problems
(gastrointestinal disorders), blood pressure disorders, asthma, and
heart disease. Psychosomatic disorders are initially functional, with no
visible physical damage, but after a while, they can lead to pathological
changes in the attacked organs.

Reincarnation
Belief in the return to the earth again. According to this doctrine, man
is born again after death – that is, his spirit is transferred to a newcomer.
This leads to a continuous life, to the immortality of the soul.

Recipient
Carrier, receiver of the message, receptor.

Record
Obviousness. A review from which it is seen that there was something,
that something happened, that something was done, kept in mind until
the ability to execute is abandoned.

Reflection
A change in the direction of the front of the wave on the touch surface
between two different media so that the front wave returns to the
medium from which it originated. Common examples are the reflection
of light, sound, and water waves. It also means thinking, judging,
considering, and passing attention to the object. Observation of the
subject and consideration of the relationship between the subject and
the object.

Reflexive Behaviour/Action
The simplest reluctant movements are reflex movements. Reflex action is the reaction of an organism without the involvement of will and consciousness. The nerve-control centres of the reflex are located in the spinal cord.

Repetition
Repeated sounds, words, or phrases without meaning in the context.

Reprogramming
Re-making the program, rearranging, redirecting.

Resocialisation
A planned and systematically programmed process of correcting socially disadvantaged attitudes, beliefs, value systems, and associative behaviour. The goal of resocialisation is to integrate or reintegrate an individual with behavioural problems in the social environment. There are various treatments and resocialisation programs that are applied in open, semi-open, or closed protection.

Ritual
Festive act or ceremonial ceremony that is held in accordance with certain given rules and with symbolic content. Rites that are followed by certain words and gestures and can be religious or worldly.

Scientology
A set of beliefs and teachings created by science fiction writer L. Ron Hubbard in 1952 as the successor to his earlier self-knowledge of diathetics. Hubbard described scientology as a religion. In 1953, he founded the Scientology Church in New Jersey.

Séance
Planned meeting of experts and clients with the aim of psychological intervention or other therapeutic action. A spiritual gathering in which the medium mediates between the present and the ghosts.

Sensationalism
A type of biased and controversial journalistic reporting that exaggerates the descriptions of certain events and topics to increase ratings or readability. Sensationalism can include reporting on generally insignificant topics and events that do not affect the wider society at all or the presentation of a relevant topic in a biased, trivial, or tabloid manner. Sensationalism can also be defined as a targeted and provoked reaction by publishing untested and incomplete but intriguing information.

Session
A meeting, congress, or symposium held in one or more days.

Siamese Twins
Identical twins whose bodies are connected to each other. They represent a rare phenomenon, and it is estimated that it is happening between one in fifty thousand or one hundred thousand births.

Sniper
A rifle fitted with an optical lens. One who uses such a rifle.

Sphere
In geometry, it represents a three-dimensional body – a ball. In sociology, it indicates the field of work, area, region, range, scope, territory.

Spiritism
Latin *spiritus*. It denotes communication with ghosts. Occult science that studies ways of communicating with deceased people.

Subconscious
A part of the human mind that is responsible for all the automatic functions of the organism. Here is where the immune system is located, and it takes care of the blood, breathing, and all other automatic body functions. The basic task and the main priority of the subconscious is survival. It performs its task by adjusting the body to what it considers

to be a reality. It has preserved 'programmed answers' to various life situations and reactions to everything that has been happening in life, preserved to serve as a model of behaviour for the basic task of the subspecies, such as security and survival. All those things that a person performs automatically, without thinking, are controlled by the subconscious. Here are your habits, both good and bad.

Symbiosis
Common life. Useful, close, and lasting community of two or more diverse organisms (symbionts) – animals and animals, animals and plants, plants and plants.

Syndrome
In the psychology of personality and social psychology, it signifies a set of empirical and meaningful related character lines that occur.

Sublimation
Latin *sublimare* (exalt, elevate). Convert to something exalted, something more. In a portable sense, it denotes idealisation.

Suggestion
The procedure of open or secret guidance by another person or group of people to accept uncritically, without compulsion, ideas, beliefs, attitudes, or certain patterns of behaviour. This conviction is manifested as an address or command. Suggestions are often used in therapy as well as in economic, political, and every other propaganda.

Theta State
It represents the state of mind in which the frequency of our mind is between four and seven titres per second (during sleep, relaxation, or meditation).

Telepathy

A word composed of the Greek words *tele* (distance) and *pathe* (feeling). Ability to exchange thoughts and feelings between two or more people remotely, without mediating media.

Teleportation

The act or process of moving an object from one place to another with the help of special skills or advanced technology.

Theory

It represents an abstract, general knowledge of a problem that is the result of search for the truth. In empirical science, a system of interconnected and aligned claims arising from the compression and generalisation of a series of partial empirical findings, as well as the integration of a number of verified facts, hypotheses, and laws relating to one realm of reality.

Trauma

From wounds or injuries (physical or mental). Psychological trauma is a very strong and unmanageable mental earthquake following a dangerous experience.

Information is everything, and everything is information. It is omnipresent energy that has the ability to transform from one form to another, regardless of space and time. As long as man tries to master it as much as possible, information is fully managed solely by the Creator.

— George Špirić Fraxon

Index

A

acupuncture 114-16, 119, 122
adrenaline 81, 223
aesthetics viii, 223, 230
Alfa Power ix
alpha 14, 23, 29-30
amnesia 48-50, 135, 140-1, 224
amoeba 25, 71, 183, 190, 224
Anaesthetic 4, 33, 35-6, 224
Anamnesis 224
animal magnetism 55, 235
anthropologist 176-7, 225
artefact 225
artificial memories 12, 146, 150, 181, 211-12
asthma 41, 225, 239
Aura 194, 198-9, 203, 209, 211, 225, 235
autosuggestion ix, 18, 22, 26-8, 34

B

Baird, James 68
beta 14, 29

biological death 125, 133-4, 136
Black, Stefan 15

C

Cardiopulmonary Resuscitation (CPR) 124, 225
Cerebral Cortex 225
cerebral death 125
chemotherapy 119-20, 226
Chi 105, 114, 119, 134
clinical death xii, 122, 124-5, 130, 132-7, 151, 226
code 50-1, 54, 93, 96, 99, 102-4, 166, 168, 180-3, 190-1, 217, 226
coherent 226
concept viii, 2, 31, 55, 167, 171-2, 174, 176-7, 185, 220, 226-7, 230-1, 236
confusion 31, 34, 38, 55, 60-1, 68, 154, 157, 210, 227, 236
consensus 54, 160, 227
continuum 158-60, 164, 227

Creator xii-xiii, 93, 96, 104, 176-8, 181-3, 191, 195, 245

D

defibrillation 124, 227
delta state 34-6
delta waves 14
dominant 32, 43, 214, 227
dysfunctional 46, 118, 227

E

egocentricity 58-60
electroencephalograph 13, 227
emotion 42, 45-6, 49, 65, 83, 141, 202, 228, 231-3, 239
Emotional Intelligence 196, 228
energy of life xv, 134, 219
engram 43-5, 228
entropy 175-7, 228
epilepsy 32-3, 41, 140, 229
Epinephrine Injection 124, 229
esoteric 225, 229
Esperanto 165, 229
ether 12-13, 27, 193-4, 197, 212, 229
ethics 161, 230
euphoria 99, 230
explanation xii, 15, 26, 31-2, 68, 72, 79, 82, 94, 96, 102, 127, 129, 153, 155-7, 159, 169, 230

F

Faraday, Michael 68
fascinating 7, 184, 230
frequency 12, 14, 161, 230, 242
frigidity 39, 44-6, 230-1

G

gene 182
genetic mutations 182, 231
Genetics 231

group hypnosis 16, 32-3
guru 37, 60, 117, 232

H

harmonisation 43, 62, 232
Hindu Veda 232
hippocampus 140-1, 232
homeopathy 108-9, 118, 232
human brain 8-9, 13-14, 25, 95, 101, 103, 139, 141-2, 146, 166, 178-81
hypnosis vii-viii, xii, 1-6, 11, 14-16, 22, 29, 31-4, 36, 52-6, 73-4, 95, 116, 118, 152, 161, 232
hypnotherapist 1, 11, 15-16, 29-30, 32, 34-6, 40-3, 55, 61, 140
hypnotherapy 4, 16, 35, 39, 41, 118, 140, 233
hypnotic anaesthesia 3, 35-6
hypnotic regression 2, 39-41, 43, 233
hysteria 33, 233

I

Implication 27, 46, 51, 233
inhibition 179, 233
intimate 42, 44-5, 233
IQ (intelligence quotient) 196, 234
irritation viii, 15-16, 88, 147, 191, 228, 231, 233

K

Kern, Otto 67

L

Loyalty 234

M

manipulation xii, 57-9, 64, 68, 70, 78, 101, 134, 168, 210, 234
marketing 18, 20-2, 33, 98, 122
mass hypnosis viii, 1-3, 5, 15-16, 33-4

medicine 4, 31-2, 43, 51, 55, 72, 87, 90, 108-9, 111, 113-14, 116-22, 125, 134, 137, 150, 156, 179, 213-14, 232, 234

meditation 11, 14, 34, 60, 106, 234, 242

medium 16, 18-19, 29-30, 70, 73, 183, 239

memory 8, 12, 23, 30, 49-50, 70, 90, 113, 134-5, 138-42, 144-8, 150-3, 162, 168, 180-2, 184, 190, 211, 214-15, 224, 228, 232, 235

Mesmer, Franz 55

mesmerism 55, 235

messiah 10, 235

Metadata 235

migraine 41, 235

Milehnjin, Anatoly 15

minor 14, 27, 119, 235

modify 236

Motive/Motivation 6, 83, 236

mystification 45, 236

myths 37, 104, 236

N

nano-particles 70, 90, 209, 236

narcissistic personality disorder 63-5

nucleotide sequence (nucleic acid) 236

O

observation 4, 54, 127, 171, 176, 194, 196, 210, 223, 236, 239

orb 72, 163, 193-203, 208-12

P

Palpation 237

paranoia 55, 101, 121, 237

Pavlov, Ivan 15

phenomenon xv, 15, 32, 45, 50, 55-6, 58, 61, 72, 74, 79-80, 84-5, 88-91, 93, 97, 116, 125, 127-9, 132-3, 135-6, 147, 153, 155-6, 159, 161, 165-7, 169, 193-4, 210-12, 227-8, 237, 241

pheromones 185, 189, 237

phobias 33, 38, 61, 237

Photosynthesis 237

physical death 94, 151

physiology 26, 114, 127, 179, 237

Pigment 49-50, 238

post-hypnotic suggestion 18, 22, 24, 31, 77, 238

potential xvi, 9-10, 56, 134, 150-2, 195, 238

practice xi, 2, 5, 9, 22, 32, 34-5, 40, 44, 47, 52, 55-6, 59, 61-2, 68-9, 71-2, 80, 83, 101, 103-4, 106, 111, 113-14, 124, 138-9, 141, 150, 155-7, 173-4, 176, 178, 180, 190, 217, 229, 238

practitioner 1, 238

prayers 11, 14, 75, 78, 122, 143-4

preliminary 44, 118, 238

profit 22, 31, 100, 122, 238

psyche 6, 26, 41, 61, 104, 239

psychics xii, 4, 26, 62, 93, 96-8, 100-1, 155

psychosomatic disorder 4, 32, 239

R

recipient 6, 18-19, 24, 80-1, 107, 172-3, 187, 237, 239

record xvi, 40, 67, 94, 98-9, 142, 147, 151-3, 169, 212, 227

reflection 72, 195-6, 209, 212, 239

reflexive 240

reflexive behaviour 240

regression therapy 38, 40, 42-3, 45, 51

reincarnation 2, 239

repetition 21, 34, 42, 240

Reprogramming 101, 240

resocialisation 6, 240

ritual viii, 31, 66, 94, 107, 112, 190, 240

S

Scientology 240

Séance 240

self-hypnosis 34

Sensationalism 100, 241

session 2, 16, 37, 43-4, 46-7, 49-50, 68,
70, 72-5, 77, 117, 121, 238, 241

sessions 2, 16, 37, 43-4, 46-7, 49, 68, 70,
74-5, 77, 117, 241

Siamese twins 241

Siamese Twins 241

sniper 48, 241

sphere 5-6, 103, 229, 234, 241

spiritism xii, 66-8, 70, 73, 77-8, 165, 241

subconscious 18-21, 25, 30-2, 89, 91-2,
152, 232-3, 241-2

sublimation 2, 16, 18-24, 33, 242

suggestion 11, 15, 17-24, 30-2, 35, 76-7,
171, 238, 242

Symbiosis 242

Syndrome 10, 37, 242

T

telepathy xii, 79-81, 83-6, 88-92, 104,
219, 243

teleportation 89-90, 92, 134, 136, 167,
179-80, 243

Tesla, Nikola ix, 9-10, 54, 70-1, 127, 150-
1, 159, 193-4

theory 52, 55, 68, 80, 83, 105, 127, 139,
153, 160, 172-6, 179, 182, 195-6,
230, 243

trauma ix, 30, 43, 49, 109, 224, 231, 243